RE-BUILDING THE RUINED PLACES

A journey out of childhood trauma

Lorraine Cavanagh

Ameo Books

ISBN: 978-1-7391567-0-1
Imprint: Ameo Books
Theatreset Ltd. Abergavenny NP78TH
A catalogue record for this book is available from the British Library

Scriptural quotations taken from NRSV Anglicized Edition 1995

My thanks to
Helen Rose Andrews, Susan Brison, Sean Cavanagh,
Serena Colchester, Tony Collins, Julia Gregson, Hannah Hale,
Katy Kelly, Bea Harmston, Joe Harmston, Polly Meynell,
Rebecca Parnaby-Rooke, Antony Pickthall, John Smyth
and to #Women Writers Network.

Each in their different ways made it possible to tell this story.

OTHER BOOKS BY LORRAINE CAVANAGH

By One Spirit: Reconciliation and Renewal in Anglican Life

The Really Useful Meditation Book

Making Sense Of God's Love: Atonement and Redemption

Finding God in Other Christians

Beginning Again: Reconnecting with Jesus Christ

Waiting on The Word: Preaching Sermons that Connect People
with God

In Such Times: Reflections on Living with Fear

He took me by the Hand (translation)

RE-BUILDING THE RUINED PLACES

This book is based on the author's experiences. In order to protect privacy, some names, identifying characteristics, dialogue and details have been changed or reconstructed.

For S and J

'They shall build up the ancient ruins, they shall raise up the former devastations; they shall repair the ruined cities, the devastation of many generations'

Is. 61:4

Contents

Introduction

To understand is to forgive. But is it always incumbent on the abuse victim to forgive their abuser? Many Christians would say that it is, but they might say this without having considered what is needed for genuine forgiveness to take place and what it is reasonable to expect from the victim. Genuine forgiveness does not mean excusing someone else's behaviour on the grounds, perhaps, that things were different then, or that the abuser did not know what they were doing. These are, at best, opaque truths. Abuse is abuse precisely because the abusers do know what they are doing, whether the abuse they are inflicting is sexual, physical, or emotional.

People of my generation who experienced abuse in childhood and early adulthood may have spent most of their lives trying to pretend that it was in some way justified or understandable. We compress and pack away our memories, along with the pain they trigger, rather than trying to arrive at a deeper and more dispassionate understanding of how the abusers came to be as they were, whether as a result of abuse they may have experienced themselves, or because it was simply accepted in those times, even in privileged families. We need to be both honest and dispassionate about the pain we experienced, and that many of us still experience through our flashbacks and memories.

I have written this book as someone who came to the Christian faith quite late in life, long after most of my abusers had died. The journey to faith, including all the dead ends I have encountered in it, has eventually landed me in a place where I can look at the trauma of my childhood dispassionately and at times even gratefully, which is not to say that I look at it without feeling. It is just that it has become fertile ground, like compost, in which I try to allow understanding to take root and grow. I hope that seeing my own experience of trauma as something that is not wasted, but has a meaning and purpose, will allow others to own and validate the pain they still experience as a result of childhood trauma, even if, as with so many women of my generation, it has remained buried for decades.

LC   June 6th, 2022

Chapter 1

Memory

'Do not remember the former things, or consider the things of old.'

Isaiah 43:18

Your life begins before the things or moments that you first remember. Even at the initial moment of sentient consciousness, we have a story to tell ourselves, a context in which to place the rest of our life. That pre-remembered context, along with our very earliest memories, will decide our life's emotional trajectory and possibly our faith trajectory as well. This is not fate. It is just that experiences teach us to recognise the fact that how we deal with what happens to us in life is conditioned by circumstances, but not pre-defined by them.

Towards the end of the Second World War, when my father had escaped from a German POW camp, he sent my mother a bottle of Jean Patou perfume. He was caught again, trying to cross the Pyrenees, and re-imprisoned in Pamplona. But he was able to send her the bottle of perfume. It was called 'Je reviens'.

I was born in 1946. My parents had been married for two years and had a son, my brother, Charles-Albert, who died in infancy. I felt a deep connection with this baby, wondering at times if I had been his replacement. But this did not in any way diminish the particular and very private love I had for this, my closest blood relative.

Long before the war, my parents had met at the famous Moulin in Ermenonville, just north of Paris, where my grandmother supported, and helped to launch, the careers of many of the most iconic artists and writers of the early twentieth century. She and her husband, Harry Crosby, ran the Black Sun Press which published some of the earliest works by D.H. Lawrence, Hart Crane and Scott Fitzgerald, among others. It is quite possible that The Great Gatsby himself was modelled on Harry Crosby.

The war, and the world my grandparents inhabited, was my pre-nascent context. The war also gave me a reason to be proud of my father. As I grew older, it would be hard to hold on to the idea of him as a father. I needed to think of him in that heroic war context, forgetting as far as possible those other moments that would press on me and shape themselves into a painful and far more insistent memory.

My earliest memory is a very mixed one. I am in the north of France, sent there to be looked after by a couple who had cared for my mother as a child. Although I have no idea why I am there, I am at peace with life, though beginning to be curious. I see, in the window of the local hardware store, what looks like a rather clumsy instrument with leather tassels on it, which I later discover is used to remove cobwebs and dust from furniture and awkward corners. I ask the person I am with what it is for. She replies that it is for beating little girls when they are naughty. There are a great many of them in the shop window, so I conclude that a great deal of beating must go on. I take it to mean that I am one of those little girls. I experience shame for the first time. I also learn, mostly by putting pieces together, that the reason I was fostered out was to allow my mother to "have some fun", as she put it. She was about to marry my first stepfather who owned a large and very beautiful yacht.

My first memory of Katrina, my half-sister, was on that yacht, a big three-masted schooner called *Freelander*. Katrina is five years younger than I am. Her father is Sir William Blythe.

I associate *Freelander* with a great deal of fear. First, there was the time when my mother had been left on the boat with the crew and her two young children. We were to sail from Gibraltar into the port of Malaga when half way on the journey a vicious squall blew up. One of the crew told me to say my prayers because we were going to drown. We could see a couple waving to us from a dinghy marooned under some cliffs which seemed very near to us, but we sailed on. I dreamed of those two people for years. I also dreamed of the drowned body we passed on another occasion in the Bay of Biscay, floating face down in the water. In Malaga harbour, the crew would amuse themselves by dangling me over the side and threatening to drop me into the black water below. The fear of this abyss, the fear of abandonment and of death itself would return to me in so many other contexts, especially religious ones.

The memory of the tasselled duster remains completely detached from other memories of that time, as do the memories of the shipwrecked couple and the drowned man. At the same time, they play into my life in subtle ways, bending and distorting my perception of what people were supposed to be like. They also distorted my own self-understanding. That first memory lodged itself in my inner psyche, so that I believed myself to be fundamentally deserving of some kind of punishment and that I was, in truth, a bad person. This was despite the rest of my early years during which I experienced nothing but kindness and love from the relatives who cared for me. They were my father's family, although my father could not bear to have anything to do with them because of the way my grandfather had behaved during the war.

My grandfather's house in Normandy, where I spent my summers, had been Rommel's headquarters. My grandfather had a housekeeper, Mademoiselle Lucie, who dressed entirely in white. He would stroke her upper thigh when he thought no one was looking. He said I looked like my grandmother who I assumed must have looked like Mademoiselle Lucie. I instinctively recoiled from him. I also learned that my grandfather could have requisitioned my father for agricultural work, knowing that he was a prisoner of war, but he did not do this. I was uncomfortable around my grandfather who I knew had failed his son by not getting him out of prison. I could never decide whether this was out of cowardice or laziness. Either way, it not only diminished him in my eyes but even at that early age, made me distrust what I sensed to be an artificial class system that defined the life style and shaped the gilded cage in which we all seemed to be living.

My American mother came from an old New England family. She was always keen to point out that the French aristocracy was based on nothing, since France no longer had a king, so the fact that I was not, in her eyes, the granddaughter of a real Marquis served as a tool for my diminishment. Nothing about me meant anything. I carried this idea on into adult life. Nothing was worth doing because I was a fake. I would ultimately fail at everything. My very existence was laughable.

I associate my earliest years in France with formal settings in which I eat at a separate table with a governess, and with the village church and a bell that sounds for the midday meal. One day I accompany my governess to the church. She says that she has to go to confession and I am to wait quietly until she has finished. I beg her to tell me what she is going to confess and she seems to be extremely troubled by my pestering her with this question. I sense that there are adult emotions swirling around about which I know nothing, but I am extremely curious about them. I want to know what they are, why they are, and what they feel like. I want to know why a person has to confess them.

At that time I associated churches with confessing your sins and with a kind of warm light visible from a distance as one sat in a dark space somewhere near the back. I began to think of this distant light as having to do with the existence of God who I would meet when I died and who would decide whether I went to Heaven or Hell. But before then it seemed that it was important to keep God on my side by telling him my sins and going to Mass on Sundays and other days, even though I felt completely detached from what went on there.

Later, going to Mass on Sundays became an absolute imperative, even though as a Catholic I grew up in an entirely agnostic home setting. My father was a Catholic and on marrying him, my mother had to promise that I would receive a Catholic education. I don't remember my parents being together. They split when I was about two years old. I was never sure why my mother kept her promise, although she seemed to be attracted to the Catholic Church. Perhaps it was the mystique of it that drew her. It may have provided a counterpoint to the occult in which she so frequently dabbled. Perhaps it afforded her some kind of protection by proxy from the influence of the 'spooks', as she called them. She never went to church herself. When they were still married, she insisted that my father attend Brompton Oratory on a Sunday while she waited for him outside. The Oratory was one of two fashionable Catholic churches in London.

Receiving a Catholic education also involved going to Sunday school where I learned that your soul could be in your little finger, or so it seemed to me from what we were being told. At school, I was told that I would go to Hell if I missed Mass on a Sunday. You were taught that Hell was an eternal experience of the pain of separation from God. I did not feel particularly close to God in the context of church, even though there was something beautiful about what went on there, so I could not envisage the pain or what this separation could possibly mean. I could not understand why being separated from such a distant God who expected so much of me, and whose expectations I could never hope to meet, should be so painful. I felt very guilty about wondering such a thing.

I also knew that it would be quite easy to miss Mass through no fault of my own, because the parent, the mother who would overshadow my childhood, was not a person of faith and did not hold with a God who would punish small children for their sins. I sensed, nevertheless, that she was perhaps afraid of something which had to do with the spiritual, but not with God. She saw ghosts, held seances and consulted Ouija boards. Our house had a chilling strangeness about it.

My mother, Polleen, was the most beautiful woman in London. Our house was full of famous people, mostly men. Some of these men stayed around long enough for us to think of them as 'stepfathers'. Katrina and I lived for much of the time apart from that world. We lived with Marge, in her small council flat. Marge had looked after my mother throughout the war and stayed on, I later realised, to watch over my sister and me. She would spend her days in our Belgravia flat and then walk us home with her. Her world was our normality. Our mother knew nothing of our whereabouts most of the time.

People came to our mother's house for drinks in the morning and the drinking went on for the rest of the day. She would often disappear for weeks, entrusting us to Marge. The reasons she gave for her absences were the same as when I was younger. She wanted to 'have fun'. She did not like to be questioned about her lifestyle or crossed in any way, especially concerning her political beliefs which we children sensed were ill informed and made all the more embarrassing by her drinking. As I grew older I realised that the drinking was a way of covering up the fact that her expensive private education in Switzerland had not equipped her for intellectual conversation with the sort of people she surrounded herself with, so she must have experienced a degree of shame in this respect. She went with politicians and intellectuals who flattered her with their attention but she understood nothing of their thinking, or of their motives in regard to her. She did not like to be challenged.

As with so many of her generation, she hid the sadness she carried within her by drinking. The drinks parties that began at around midday would eventually extend themselves into hours of solitary drinking throughout the rest of the day and on into the night. I experienced the shame of her alcoholism, but I also felt something of its pain. She had lost the two men she had really loved to the war. She had lost my brother, and had had countless abortions, or so she claimed with a degree of pride. She covered much of her sadness with obdurate pride, and with rage, and she fed both with gin. "Get me a drink, darling, to steady my nerves" she would say when faced with anything resembling a challenge to her opinions or when she was feeling generally unsettled. I would try to get away with putting less and less gin in the glass and greater quantities of ice, in an effort to slow down the effect that the gin would have on her personality. But she was never too drunk not to notice this small subversive act. "Cat's piss" she would call it and then remix the drink herself.

She was angry on one much later occasion because I would not take her with me to the convent near where we lived, because she was drunk and smelled of gin. She poured herself another drink, but misjudged the tap pressure and was showered with water. I experienced a petty but pleasing sense of retribution, and then tried hard to forgive, not yet realising that forgiveness does not involve trying.

I thought a lot about forgiving, and about being forgiven, especially when it came to my mother's drinking. I wanted her to be forgiven for the shame I endured when she walked down the street defiantly with a drink in her hand, announcing that she was "just a little bit drunk". Forgiving and being forgiven seemed so closely enmeshed, given how religious people talked about forgiveness, but forgiveness did not seem to fit in the emotional landscape I grew up in, or that my mother would inhabit for most of my adult life. I did not know what it felt like to forgive, or to receive forgiveness, although I was taught to ask for it when I prayed. I was also given to believe that my parents and 'stepfathers' were above reproach. This presumably meant that although they caused my sister and me great pain, they were not in need of our forgiveness, or of anyone else's. Our mother took the position of never being wrong about anything. No adult was ever wrong about anything. Nothing concerning how I later felt about my relationship with my stepfather and those who protected him was spoken of, not even by Marge.

Everyone was afraid of something, it seemed, but nothing was said. I was also afraid to own the pain and the memories that were vaguely associated with this general sense of secrecy and fear. The two did not always fit together well and they would, in any case, have been denied, had I spoken of them to anyone. I would have been told not to be silly. But there was something hard lodged inside me, all the same, something I was meant to forgive but could not give a name to. It was a kind of hard sadness.

As a Catholic, and as a child, I also had to find whatever it was in myself that needed forgiving, that required that I go to confession. It was almost a given that the sins I 'confessed' would need to be insignificant, since I did not want to alarm the priest who was hearing my confession. I did sometimes wonder if it would not be more interesting for him if I were to confess something that was really sinful, like wishing my mother was dead, but that would be deserving of Hell and eternal punishment. It would be good to confess that sin perhaps, to say what I really felt in the anonymity of the confessional, but better to exercise caution. So I returned the sin to the place where the hard sadness lived.

It was not just eternal punishment that I feared, when it came to sin and God, but something much more immediate that had to do with severance and separation. If there was to be any kind of meaningful separation from God, it must, I thought, feel like the pain I experienced when my mother came to remove me from my father's family who fostered me in my early years, my aunt Aude and my cousin Natalie. I lived with them in their large apartment in Paris which smelled of *pot pourri* and furniture polish. They took me with them when they went to my aunt's house near Bourges where I had my adored pony, 'Goliat'. 'Goliat' was a small Shetland who taught me how to stay on a horse, no matter how challenging the circumstances, though not necessarily with any degree of elegance.

I remember drowning in darkness as the taxi drew further away from the street in Paris when my mother came to get me. She was embarrassed by my crying. "Don't be silly, darling" she had said. I would remember the anguish of the moment for the rest of my life.

So much of early childhood involves making sense of the pain of separation. Is separation something inevitable, like separating an animal from its young? Is it truly necessary? I was given to understand that it was, but I did not believe it. How was it that other children were not sent away to boarding school? At the same time, and as the years went by, coloured by the regular separations of being sent away from home, I did not feel I was being separated from love itself, but from contexts in which love should have been the defining feature. There was always something missing in our home environment. There was a vacuum, an emptiness. This sense of vacuum would return in later life, every time I had to leave a familiar place, or end a relationship. It was a great sense of nothingness, of leaving nothing in order to go nowhere, of being nothing. As a child, I came home from staying with friends with an acute sense of this absence of any kind of defining contour to my life, and of re-entering a dark place, an empty and disturbing context. Our house was not like theirs. There were rooms we dared not go into alone, where plants and objects would be found to have been disturbed in a mysterious way, where curtains moved of their own accord and where a silhouetted woman walked through the wall into my mother and stepfather's bathroom. No one would tell us who she was.

It was also a context in which I did not fully belong. Being the step-child, I had a different name to everyone else. It was French and did not pronounce well in English. My mother would use it to bring me down by inferring that my appearance – untamed hair and general gawkiness – fell far short of what it should be, given my name, which she pronounced in such a way as to make it sound almost royal. I did not live up to the name. Neither did I share, or live up to, my stepfather's name. In such an unbounded emotional climate, and with such a blurred sense of identity, I did not know if I belonged anywhere, or to any one person, so I learned to make the best of things.

*

There are so many human relationships which hold together by making the best of things, opting to stay in and see it through. Adults are often, but not always, in a position to make a choice about whether they do this. As an adult, if you do not belong in a given context, you generally leave. But a child is powerless in this respect. The difference for children growing up with abuse, whether it is psychological, sexual or spiritual, or a combination of all three, lies in their being unable to make any choice about their circumstances, because they are not free to leave and they have little or no power to change things. This feeling of powerlessness then colours the way they live their lives and the way they think about faith and God.

The nearest I got to leaving was being allowed to walk or cycle to Mass on Sundays. I usually went on my own, since no one at home was a Catholic. Just being there in the church gave me a brief sense of identity. Once there, I also felt a curious sense of peace. Although I was a lone seven-year-old sitting in a pew near the front, I felt I belonged. People, when they noticed I was there, were kind to me, until the collection plate came round and I thought they were offering me some money and gratefully helped myself to a fistful of shillings and sixpences. They never asked my name.

It became increasingly hard to place God, who was after all the God of Love, into the disparate contexts of school, church and home, and to understand that the way we children were treated at home, and the way we were taught to think about God at school, was part of God's purpose, of his 'will'. At the same time, I learned to accept the sense of separation and general lostness that I experienced both at home and at school, so I accepted God as part of what was happening to me. Yet, like Dostoevsky's Ivan, who is horrified by the way cruelty to a small child seems acceptable to God, I was tempted to 'return him the ticket'.[1] I wanted to be free of the constraints of Catholicism and I sensed that life would be so much simpler if I did not believe in God. Few adults I knew had any kind of faith and it seemed to me that their lives were freer and happier as a result. They were not afraid of what would ultimately happen to them if they were not Catholics or, worse still, did not believe in God or pray. I would like to have returned God the ticket. At the same time, I dared not do this. Although God's rationale of goodness, and the salvation that we were taught to believe in, made no sense at all in my universe, I accepted it unquestioningly.

This acceptance was reinforced in equal measure by non-religious parents on the one hand, and by a highly religious

---

[1] *The Brothers Karamazov* Taken from Ivan's dialogue with his brother, Alyosha, who is preparing to become a monk

school environment on the other. At my convent boarding school we thought a great deal about God, although I do not remember being actually taught to pray. We were very afraid of the nuns, especially of the nun who could 'freeze' a room full of little girls simply by entering it. I often wondered how she prayed when she was alone with God and concluded that since she was a nun, she was setting us an example of the kind of God we were supposed to pray to; remote and yet disturbingly seductive. Chapel was redolent with the sensory delights of incense and polished wood, but God did not seem to be a God who identified with our immediate needs, or with the real questions we were asking. For some of us, the most significant of these pertained to making sense of our abandonment by our parents and of the innate unworthiness inculcated through the religious teaching we received at school, which was reinforced at home.

In the case of parental upbringing, it was not so much a matter of being told that our world was a perfect one, but of being dismissed as delusional or 'brain washed' if I dared to suppose that it was anything other than perfect. In such a formative environment a person's understanding of what is true or not true, real or imagined, becomes clouded. I would conclude that it was more likely that I was in some way wrong, even though my instincts, and the occasional adult (including the therapists I was sent to stay with because I was so difficult) might imply that I was not. As a result, I lived with a sense of guilt, that perhaps I was failing to appreciate my mother for who she really was, the beautiful, talented and witty person so adored by her friends. I should be proud to have Polleen as a mother, and, in a way, I was. She, and the men she surrounded herself with, were at the epicentre of the sophisticated adult world we could hear going on behind closed doors, where people came for drinks in the morning and returned again later that evening, a world of heavily scented flowers and elegant drawing rooms, of dinners and parties, of clever quips and whispered asides.

We, who boasted of being part of that glamorous world, were the envy of our school friends, but it was a hard profile to maintain and I did not, in any case, believe it. I pretended to be proud of my mother and of the current stepfather, or of whatever man was currently in favour. I wanted to be like them, but I was trying to be someone I knew I could never be, have something that would never be mine. I was simply not that person. I had hair that was too curly and I wore special shoes to correct my feet. I did not belong in that place. I did not look the part.

God was becoming increasingly opaque in regard to all these conflicting feelings. While I sensed a vague solidarity coming from God in regard to who I really was, and some of the feelings I experienced, I felt none of this in regard to how I could make myself into someone my mother would be proud of, beginning with changing the way I looked. God was seldom discernible in all the vague longings to be someone else, to be thin, to have straight hair and a 'normal' life, even though I did not really know what this normality consisted of or where to look to find it.

Faith, and prayer itself, was bound and circumscribed by these inarticulate longings and the grief they caused. Grief was tied to fantasy but, as I later learned, in order for grief to bear fruit, to become something that will in some measure serve others, you have to have known what you are grieving for and what you have lost. If you are told that your grief is unfounded, that the pain of separation that you experience is either imagined or fabricated, you grieve in a vacuum. In other words, you try to banish the cause of grief from your active memory in an effort to accept that the unhappy circumstances you find yourself in are not unhappy at all. I even became quite a 'happy' child. I laughed a lot. I wanted to appear normal because the grief I carried was too precious and too fragile to be shared with anyone. I was also acutely sensitive to anything that felt like diminishment or criticism, a hypersensitivity that would remain with me for most of my life. I did not want advice, or to be told anything about myself by anyone, least of all by people close to me who I felt had betrayed me. I trusted no one.

As a child, I found it hard to distinguish between those who might betray me, even unwittingly, and those who would not. So I tried to stay safe by keeping up the appearances of normality and happiness. But I also knew that I would not be able to do this indefinitely. The fragile ramparts that I had constructed around myself would not hold forever against the rising tide of my anger and self-doubt. At some point I was going to be faced with the fact that these defences were not impregnable. They would not hold up when the only love that really matters came along. I sensed the possibility of that love being out there somewhere, but I did not understand what it was, assuming it to be about some kind of idealised relationship of completely requited love with a man. I would sometimes project this persona onto the men who surrounded my mother. I would occasionally fall in love with one of them. They seemed to be the kind of men one should look to be marrying. But I also sensed something else, deeper, more constant, more total that would require everything of me, a kind of journey's end where someone quite 'other' waited for me. I felt this person, who I had no name for, had expectations of me and I feared I would never meet them. It seemed that the love in question was somehow connected to praying, but not to the Catholic Church. I was both worried and fascinated. There was an inevitability about it all, as if, sooner or later, this compelling love would catch up with me.

*

Later I would recognise these tentative brushes with love for what they were, brushes with the love of God, and my resistance to them as a struggle against salvation itself. I would also learn, painfully, of the way truth functions, not as a set of propositions to which I must acquiesce, but as the experience of having been loved for who and what I am, even when I did not know this was happening. During the course of this process I would learn that there is no such thing as pointless suffering in the economy of God. No life is ever a waste, no matter how great the mess a person may have made of it. This is not to say that all grief, and all suffering, are part of God's purpose, that they are somehow willed on us, but that from the moment a person is able to learn real faith, they begin to see grief and suffering being 'worked' into a new creation. They begin to see something of the meaning of the Cross of Christ. We can either go with the grain of the wood of the Cross and allow God to work with our pain, or work against it through resistance or outright denial.

It took me many years to understand that I had to stop resisting, that I must go back to where the grief was first experienced and know the abuse again for what it was, rather than continue to deny it in the way I had been conditioned to do and which would make life superficially easy and less complicated. The person I once was had been shaped through a denial of who I really was, which is a person worthy of God's love and of the love of my parents. The lies that I was fed were therefore a kind of blasphemy. They disfigured my sense of self and they disfigured the face of God.

The cynical disfigurement of any victim of abuse is a disfigurement of the very image of God that we bear within ourselves. But the image of God is not so easily effaced, perhaps because it is most often discernible in suffering. There is a scarlet thread that runs through every life. It is the colour of the blood of Christ. When we see it for what it is, it reveals itself as a life force, acting in our psyche like a transfusion. It courses through our memories, replacing the old thin de-oxygenated blood of the past with the oxygen of life that enables courage.

Courage is what the victim of any form of abuse most needs. They need the courage to remember the truth of what they have experienced and the truth of what they are now. So they need to remember aright. My own experience has taught me that the truth about abuse has to do with those moments that we remember most clearly, because they are the moments that have wounded us most. They may be insignificant to others and easily brushed aside by both the abuser and their victims, but it is the pain of them that marks a person and, in their own mind, disfigures them. What little psychotherapy I received gave me a truth to believe in, chiefly that I was not a liar or a 'problem'. It was my parents who were the problem. To hear someone say this for me gave me permission to own this truth for myself. I stayed with Joan and K, the therapists I had been sent to, for a week. I should have remained with them for three months, but my father, who until then had made only occasional appearances in my life, was sent from Paris to forcibly remove me when it was decided that I was being 'brainwashed'. The enduring agony of that separation remained with me for years and I can recall it at will, as if it were yesterday. I owe Joan and K my life because they taught me not to be afraid of the truth, to hold fast to it, to remember aright.

Remembering aright requires courage, because it also requires that we imagine what shapes the actions and thinking of those who abuse us, how they came to be what they are. This is not the same thing as excusing or explaining their behaviour with a view to justifying it. Truth does not explain things away. It puts our memories in sharper perspective, the better for us to understand our pain and the way it is often consciously and deliberately inflicted by the abuser as a means of hiding from theirs, or as a kind of pay back for what they suffered in their own early years. But you cannot avenge the past through the past, only through the present and through those closest to you.

The narcissistic parent may herself have experienced something of what she is inflicting on her daughter, as my mother did. She may have been diminished in some way, perhaps in exactly the way she diminishes her daughter. She may or may not have been the victim of sexual abuse, but she will have experienced her own abuse with equal intensity. It may not have penetrated her body, but it will have penetrated her soul, her very self. The abuser as victim is almost always a very damaged and angry self, often imprisoned in the earliest stages of human emotional development. There is, of course, nothing her daughter can do to make up for the damage done to her mother, still less repair it. So the daughter allows herself to be held in some measure responsible for it.

My own mother had grown up in the Paris of the twenties, surrounded by wealth, eccentric artists and a stepfather who was found dead, as a result of a suicide pact with another woman. Polleen had been deeply in love with him throughout her childhood. He fed her champagne and wrote love letters to her at school. She needed that attention and went on needing what her own mother never gave her, punishing her children for the emotional deprivation of her own childhood. She wanted us to pay for something. She needed our sympathy. She would imply that her life had been so much harder than ours. Everything associated with us seemed to be in some way burdensome to her. "I had such a difficult pregnancy with you. It was a long and painful labour. I could have died," I would hear her say about my birth. I felt ashamed and guilty about this. I also allowed it to justify in some measure the often vicious put downs and general diminishments of my own few achievements, trying ever harder to win her love by aiming higher and being more generally noticeable.

In such a situation my efforts were doomed to fail because, in regard to my mother and stepfather, I had already failed simply by existing. Although I was fairly intelligent, but didn't know it, I would find that when I offered something I had made or written, these things would be tossed aside. "I'm not having that ridiculous object on my Christmas tree," my mother would say.

I was conditioned to failure. When I invited my mother to come to a rehearsal of a play in which I was performing, her presence annihilated my sense of self, so that every aspect of the performance was a failure. It took years to discover that my real problem lay with the fact that I made her feel threatened, as did my extremely beautiful sister. The parent who feels threatened by the talent, personality or beauty of a daughter will instinctively try to demolish her by destroying her daughter's sense of self.

*

How we remember the past, and thus think about the present and the future, is informed by how we have come to think of ourselves, of how we make sense of what we were told to believe we were and who we gradually realise we really are. Many people live their entire lives trying to make sense of this unequal equation, one that their memories tell them can never be fully righted.

This realisation, that I would never come to a proper sense of who I really was, brought me to a kind of crossroads in my own faith-life journey. I realised that I could not repair my damaged sense of self alone. Having had only a very brief experience of therapy, I did not have the means to do the necessary repair work, although my stay with Joan and K had been just long enough for me to receive and accept help in coming to terms with the truth; that I was, until then, living a lie in regard to who I really was and who was at fault for my general state of unhappiness. Having the therapy so abruptly stopped meant that I was essentially back on my own, nursing my still wounded self, angry with both my parents in ways that I did not fully understand and had never before experienced. I was also angrily indifferent to a God who I felt had played a part in all the lying, and kept me submissive and fearful in regard to his place in my life. I felt I had unmasked him and determined to have nothing more to do with him, or with the Church.

As I saw it, it was possible to be both angry and indifferent to God. Scripture tells us that anger is infinitely preferable to plain indifference (Rev. 3:15-16). When we have suffered abuse, it is also possible to work this anger into the way we think of God and how we remember him from earliest childhood. We may have very unformed ideas about spirituality and about the Church, but suddenly, having broken free of both (as I did shortly after leaving school), anger feels justifiable. As a former Catholic, I was beginning to connect with my wounded and outraged self through anger, privately directed at God. Furthermore, since the book of Revelation seemed to justify anger coming *from* God, it seemed only fair that I should be allowed to respond in kind.

I needed to hit back at something, so I blamed God for all the wasted years, the stolen childhood. What I was also blaming God for was the denial of the truth, a denial which prevented me from directing my anger against those who really deserved it. I did not have the courage for that, because I was afraid of being called a liar, so I was angry with myself as well. I imagined how things might have been, had I confronted my abusive parental figures with the truth about my feelings and, had I dared to own and share with some trustworthy other, the truth about what was really going on at home.

Chapter 2

Loss

'Deliver me, O Lord, from evildoers; protect me from those who are violent'

Psalm 140:1

Each summer we were sent to Deal on the East Kent coast with Marge, who continued to feed us out of her own wage packet when the money sent by our mother had run out. There were unexploded mines on the beach and we wove stories around them. Might there also be corpses buried there?

Those who don't get help with their memories have to find a place to bury them, like a murdered corpse. Bad memories have no life-giving potential. Burying them renders that part of a person's life memory dead. Whatever was good and true gets buried along with everything else leaving you with what the bible calls 'a trackless waste', on which to plot your life journey, an emotional place without the defining context of normal familial life in which to build and conserve good memories. This being said, my particular trackless waste was not without its defining structure. There was a rhythm and continuity to life, the loneliness and boredom of school, punctuated by holidays. Especially noticeable was the mark, or track, made by Marge during those long summer holidays.

All stories have a redemptive thread, a track running through them, if we keep doing the remembering by refusing to accept lies, or to play along in the deceptive games that give them credence, focusing instead on the persons who, unexpectedly perhaps, proved to be saviours. These people work the work of salvation into the lives of those around them. They become Christ figures, although they might not think of themselves in this way. Marge was such a person, a dour Scot always true to who she was and to her working-class roots. She had been born and raised in the North. Her father had been a chauffeur for a wealthy family and her mother was 'in service'. Marge herself trained as the 'under nanny' for that same family. As a young girl, she witnessed ease and gentility by day. By night and on her days off, she witnessed violence, principally from her father who regularly beat his children with a leather belt.

Marge exemplified the enduring nature of the Cross, its refusal to abandon us in its wordless confrontation of untruth.

Marge did not speak a great deal. She smoked a lot and drank quantities of tea. She rarely drank alcohol. She taught us to laugh at life, but inwardly she was angry. Sometimes I sensed this anger in her laughing and, inevitably, interpreted her wry jokes at my expense as her not taking my pain seriously enough. But I learned to laugh through that as well. More importantly, I learned mercy. There was always room for mercy in Marge's wry Scot humour. She found ways of laughing with people, even those with whom she was angry. She helped me to do the same when I was angry with myself or with my mother, but she never denied my anger.

She was obdurate in her kindness. She gave us permission to be true to ourselves. The Cross, as we see it in the lives of certain people, is obdurate. It refuses to change or blend in for convenience sake. Marge lived that kind of sacrificial life. She was able to live with integrity, in the midst of everything that was unjust and untrue. She was always true to herself and so modelled for us the meaning of integrity and the price of courage.

At times I thought she compromised her values, the values instilled in her by her working-class parents, in order to remain with us. She made excuses for the other adults, some of whom I knew she held in contempt. I thought she was being hypocritical at the time, not realising her abhorrence of hypocrisy and every form of pretence. She respected, but was never subservient to, Dad (my stepfather), my father ('the Count', as she called him) or to our mother. She had little time for our grandmother who, coming from an old Boston family, had 'let the side down' by the transparent selfishness of her hedonistic and expensive lifestyle, which cost her two family fortunes. Marge respected money for what it was and for what, in her mind, it was intended; to pay for the necessities of life and to provide for your children. She did not like Brenda, Dad's fourth wife, who had been with us in various guises for as long as we could remember.

Brenda had originally been Dad's secretary and continued as his secretary, cook, personal minder and general housekeeper after he married her. In Marge's view, having married my stepfather and acquired a title, she had crossed a line by betraying her middle class roots. Brenda gave herself what Marge called 'airs'. Marge, one sensed, expected people to know and accept themselves well enough not to have to try to become that person, or any person, by leaning too heavily on a class system for which we children sensed she had little respect. My father, 'the Count', felt the same way about people who he would describe as 'always trying to climb into the class they were born into'. Like Marge, he hated pretence. He liked people who were content with being who they were, who did not have the kind of social insecurities which turned them into manipulative bullies.

In all of this, Marge was largely silent about her feelings in regard to the people around us. It was part of the price she paid in order to remain with us. The person who lives the Cross will sometimes pay a price for their silence. They will be judged for it, often unfairly. Marge had no choice but to remain silent about the abuse I experienced from my stepfather because speaking out would have meant her leaving us, and she knew she could not do that. For my part, I understood this and simply trusted that Katrina was not enduring Uncle William, as I at first called him, in the way I was.

My father resented Uncle William, especially when the time came for me to call him Dad. The new name was given to me to use, probably to make me feel part of the family, although I was constantly reminded that I was not a Blythe. Not knowing who you really are, in regard to the powerful adults who overshadow your life, blurs any faint familial lines, any tracks that might have been drawn in the emotional waste land that you inhabit. Marge would try to set me on a firmer footing by reminding me of my own father and speaking of him in an affectionate way, while occasionally reminding me that "they don't want you either", a remark meant kindly but one which confused me and which I found difficult to come to terms with. It remained with me though, along with other occasional barbs sticking up out of the trackless waste of those emotionally inert childhood years. We played, we laughed, we went on picnics, but I was never clear where, or to whom, I belonged.

These are the years that are meant to be protected. Perhaps being left for weeks on end with Marge on a windswept and virtually uninhabited stretch of the East Kent coast was a protection of sorts, although I am not sure what it is that we were being protected from. We were only too aware of the realities around us and of the way we interfered with the grown-up world. Children were a nuisance. They marred the smooth patina of elegance and sophistication with their childish needs and importunate demands on a time that was meant to be enjoyed by adults alone. Children could be alarmingly wise at times and this made them vaguely threatening. They had it in them to blow the cover off and reveal something of the underbelly of all this subterfuge and sophistication, the *doubles ententes* that we, presumably innocent children, were not supposed to appreciate, the brittle tinkling coldness of it all. I did not get the feeling that childhood innocence, as it is commonly understood, was valued. On the other hand, we were surprisingly naïve about matters of life and death. We knew nothing of procreation and only one death figured vaguely in our landscape: Dad's sister had been killed by an unexploded land mine. I connected the memory of this death not only with the explosion of the mine but with his sudden cold rages.

My first memory of Dad, my stepfather, was one of rage. A childish tantrum of mine, having to do with not wanting to eat a boiled egg, sent him into a paroxysm of white rage. I froze. I remained deeply afraid of him for the rest of his life. There was a tremor of rage when he cautioned us about not playing with pieces of metal that we might find half buried in the sand. His grief at the loss of his sister fed his rage, or the two were at least bound up with each other. I also sensed another connection between his rage and grief, a fear of not being in control, or of not being able to control others. There was a weakness about it, a weakness that betrayed itself in later violence.

The thoughts and feelings this brought to my religious thinking were confused and contradictory. I think male weakness, especially when overlaid by anger, sows the seeds of resentment in the mind of a yet to mature Christian. The two do not fit together and they are at odds with the male God prototype which we are conditioned to believe in. Until you learn the real meaning of the 'wrath' of God as passionate grief, rather than raw anger, you secretly believe that God is, like so many angry males, fundamentally weak.[2] The thinking child will try to square this weakness with the manger and the Cross, but the two theological concepts seem to bear no relationship to each other so that the emergent religious conscience is increasingly uncomfortable with the primitive deity it has been taught to believe in.

These early experiences of male anger were also a kind of premature transition into adulthood, long before I could understand or deal with adult emotions of rage and pain. Perhaps it is at such transitional moments that the child understands how they belong in the continuum of history, in a far wider and more dangerous context over which they have no control. They are part of someone else's story and it is perhaps precisely at this moment that they learn whether the part they play in it was necessary or even wanted. Where a child knows itself to be wanted and loved, rage will ultimately be quelled by that knowledge, although the child's fear of rage itself, and what it is capable of doing to them and to others, will never quite disappear. I still find male anger deeply disturbing, whatever form it takes. But adult rage can also tell the child quite clearly that he or she does not belong

---

[2] For a development of the idea of the wrath of God as passionate grief, see my *Making Sense of God's Love: Atonement and Redemption*, (London: SPCK, 2011)

here, is not wanted, is resented, that they don't belong in anyone's story.

Most of my childhood was spent wondering if I was part of anyone's story. Did I belong in France? Or in England? At the same time, I sensed that Dad's rage was born of grief, about his own childhood, perhaps, and the strictures placed upon it by the class he was born into. He grew up on one of the family estates. He spoke of being made to run around the ballroom of the great house, to dry off after a bath. He was sent to a notoriously tough boarding school and then to naval college.

My own father grew up in a world with footmen and people who waited on you at table. One of the kindest people I remember as a small child was Giorgio who served us at mealtimes. He helped me as I grappled with over-sized silver serving utensils and did so with such grace. "Voulez-vous que je vous sers, mademoiselle?" Would you like me to serve you? It was a Christ encounter. I was humbled by it but not embarrassed. All I could say, as I still say when I hear that same gracious offer being made through the words of others, or in the silence of a moment's trust in Christ, was "Oui, s'il vous plaît". Yes, if you please. We learn prayer intuitively through the graciousness of other human beings. God teaches prayer as an expression of our dependency on, or gratitude for, grace.

We expect to learn prayer as a kind of formation which takes place at a time, or place, of innocence. When I think of both my father's and my stepfather's childhoods, I am not sure whether there is such a thing as childhood innocence, because innocence would seem to imply a lack of knowledge. They both grew up with privilege, and were conditioned to expect it, but each of them learned through life experience and through war what it meant to earn, not money, but the respect of those who mattered to them. They were conditioned by their upbringing to earning, as well as giving, respect. There was a kind of sharp underlying knowledge acquired in a privileged childhood about the reality of life in all its hardness. They understood this reality but they could not allow the truth of how it had emotionally damaged them in their particular class context. They could not own the damage or learn wisdom from it. True wisdom was hidden from them, overlaid, it seemed, with a brittle shell that protected them from learning the only knowledge worth having, the knowledge that we are loved unconditionally for who we are. The fear underlying the anger was, for both of them, driven by a greater fear of being known and loved unconditionally, or so it seemed to me as I reflected on it in later years.

The way innocence is portrayed in Genesis is misleading. Human emotional development is not innocent. It begins with the need to survive, or with what Richard Dawkins calls the selfish gene. We cease to be innocent from the moment we fear that something or someone threatens our survival, and from this fear comes every kind of aggression and idolatry. So if we are to speak of innocence we can only speak of it in terms of redemption, of how we become fully human only from the moment that we cease to fight in order to survive, that we let go and entrust our survival to the Other. Then, in weakness and often in the pains of childhood betrayals, we are made ultimately strong. But we have to travel through the weakness first. We have to live with the lies and usually believe them, before we can confidently reject them. Another way to say this is to say that we are made strong in our woundedness, in the emotional and sometimes physical battering we receive at the hands of life.

Discernment is learned as we transition from childhood to maturity. It often involves coming to terms with untruthfulness. For the person who experiences abuse, coming to terms with untruthfulness can involve one of a number of things. Truth can be denied and buried, only to be resuscitated later through various memory triggers which then demand an explanation from oneself, about how we were so weak as to allow the event to take place at all, and then from others. It can be confronted with the help of therapy, as well as with daring to confront the actual abuser, if that person is still alive and their victims have the courage to brave the accusations levelled at them by others.

When I once confided in Brenda that I would like to do this, she replied that it would be "too cruel", as if speaking the truth to my mother about the things she chose to ignore would have been the enactment of some kind of pitiless revenge. It was a mistake to confide in Brenda whose insecurities, perhaps the result of her own experience of abuse, made her fickle and manipulative, especially in regard to Katrina and me.

Looking back on all this, I know that I did not want to take revenge on anyone, but I did want justice. Justice, in the aftermath of abuse, is about being prepared to take responsibility for the truth. All parties to the abuse, including the victims, need to do this, if there is to be genuine forgiveness and healing. We start by taking responsibility for ourselves in whatever abuse we have experienced. This is not to say that we blame ourselves. Indeed, the hardest lesson any abuse survivor has to learn is that it was not their fault. They are in no way to blame, even if their relationship with the abuser was so distorted as to make them think that they, the victim, were the cause of it. But there is a sense in which we are complicit in the abuse when we simply allow it to be absorbed into our general moral landscape, telling ourselves that this is simply the way things are, or were, meant to be. In the case of historic abuse, we may tell ourselves that things were like that in those days – *autres temps, autres moeurs* – but this does not excuse us from the responsibility we bear to ourselves, and hence to our children, to own the truth about the abuse and to find what help we can to heal it. If we do not confront the truth in ourselves, if we do not confront denial, we will not learn to recognise its damaging effects on the way we may raise our own children in the future. They will, in some way, become part of our own unhappy story. We will also be less able to help others confront the truth about their actions and attitudes. It is always fear that prevents truth telling, and thus stalls the whole process of forgiveness.

I remember being with our mother when she was hospitalised after a fall and semi-conscious in A & E. I stood by her, repeating over and over again the words "I forgive you." They meant nothing, either to me or to her, because nothing had ever been said about what it was that I was actually trying to forgive. We were all too afraid to talk about it. I was afraid of being called a liar and a fantasist. She was afraid of the truth itself, of the turbulent emotions that come when someone who has experienced abuse becomes themselves an abuser; the guilt, the sense of injustice about it all. Later, when she was still unconscious, but had been moved to a side ward, a close friend came to see her and I found that I was able to 'confess' to this person, as my mother lay there stretched out between the two of us, some of the pain I had experienced, especially the way she would make a point of valuing her friends' children and their achievements, in marked contrast to anything either Katrina or I had ever done with our lives. I sensed my mother could hear what I was saying. I felt bad about the way she was not in a position at that moment to either deny or resist it, but I was grateful for that too. She was not in a position to make light of what I was saying. But she also could not ask for the forgiveness I so wanted to give her.

One thing this experience taught me is that forgiveness, for most of us, needs to be asked for. Something concrete needs to be said by someone. Unless you are an exceptionally holy person, the whole process of forgiveness needs a 'jump start', something to shock it into life. If you have suffered emotional or physical abuse something is needed from the other person, to start the process. It is not good enough to speak about abuse in generalised ways, still less to talk vaguely of the Christian duty to forgive. That simply adds insult to injury. It may be that truth needs to be heard from third parties who were, willingly or unwillingly, complicit. Speaking forgiveness to these collaborators, when they ask for it, can help the person who has experienced abuse to do the work of forgiveness in regard to the primary abuser. Third parties, as well as competent therapists and pastors, can help the forgiveness process, but they are rarely in a position to bring the abuser to a place of knowing their need for forgiveness and so begin the process of healing. This became the final chapter of my father's story. He began forgiving and accepting forgiveness with the help of the Catholic priest who heard his confession before he died.

When my father was dying, I received a phone call from a family friend asking me to come to him immediately. I was living in New York at the time, working for a charitable foundation. My boss, who could hear the conversation from the adjoining office, was already organising a plane ticket before I had put the phone down. For a moment, I was reminded of Giorgio, who had 'served' me so graciously all those years ago and saved me from my childish anxiety and potential embarrassment. My boss's efficient discretion was another example of this discreet graciousness.

I arrived at my father's bedside in time for him to take my hand and say the words "I'm sorry." It was forgiveness asked for and simply given. It was all that needed to be said. From that moment on, my memories of my father, in regard to his relationship with me, were radically changed, as were, much later, my ideas about God and about Christ. The business of forgiveness is not as hard as I thought it would be. It requires very little of us, only that we should be open to its possibility.

Our mother recovered from her fall, but there was something different in the way she behaved towards me. I believe she heard the conversation I had with her friend as we both sat by her bedside, unsure as to whether she would regain consciousness. I think I wanted her to hear it because I wanted to give her the chance of receiving forgiveness from me. She had never known how to be sorry, because it is likely that no one had ever acknowledged, let alone apologised for, the abuse she had experienced as a child. She became more considerate, a little less brittle. It was a small acknowledgment of truth, a tiny gesture of responsibility, a hint of her recognising a possible need for forgiveness.

Coming to terms with untruthfulness involves God. It does not always involve prayers, or any words at all. It is perhaps best done in a silent confrontation of God with the fact that I am a living being. I found my way of doing this by spending time in front of a life size, very beautifully carved image of the crucified Christ.[3] The truth of my situation was, and still is, reflected back to me in the kindness of the face of Christ. Sometimes, I see my father's face in his, a sure sign that all is

---

[3] The cross in the chapel of Ty Mawr Convent, Lydart, Monmouthshire.

well with my father. It deepens the bond of forgiveness which now binds us together. The Christ I am looking at is not a writhing agonised figure. It is a figure of authority, at peace with pain, giving the person contemplating him permission to own the fulness of their own pain and be at peace with it. It has enabled me to manage my anger without suppressing it or, as so many Christians mistakenly do, trying to redirect it at Christ himself. It allows me to contemplate both the pain and the forgiveness as a fact, an entity that has grown into my life.

I have yet to find this place of equilibrium with the memories I have of my stepfather, of his underlying rage, and of the sexual abuse I later endured from him. It is the rage that constantly returns, his and, to some extent, my own. We discover our own rage as we grow further into childhood and have to decide how best to manage it. I sensed in Dad an undercurrent of rage that erupted from time to time when things were not being done, or people were not behaving as they should, according to his standards. These standards were, I sensed, binary. There was a set of standards which had to do with what was expected of people, his close family and those who worked for him. He had the aristocrat's profound respect for people who did work that he valued and could understand. His friendship and respect for Kevin, the chief engineer who oversaw the fine tuning of his second yacht (engine-driven rather than sail), was probably the most profound and enduring of any he had ever known. He had a set of conflicting standards, if that is what they could be called, for women. There were women who were useful to him, like Brenda, and there were women like my mother who was beautiful, spoiled and American, whom he loved to have in the drawing room but otherwise had little time for. There were women who amused him and seduced him, including the occasional au pair. He liked clever women, but not clever children. I was deemed not to be clever, so I posed no threat to Brenda. My mother had said that I was ginger and stupid, like my father. I never heard Dad speak well of Katrina's acceptance at Oxford to read medicine. Dad did not like independent women, so to praise a woman for anything other than her looks, or potential sex appeal, was to indulge her unnecessarily.

Brenda was useful to him. He was probably violent with her. Her face often looked puffy and tearful. She had grown up with a powerful, clever and possibly violent father. She resented her role as stepmother, secretary and cook, even though she had married a title. She also resented Katrina, Dad's real daughter, rather than his tolerated stepdaughter. Katrina was both clever and beautiful. Brenda's malice and vicious outbursts of temper directed at Katrina betrayed her own feelings of insecurity in regard to her education and her general place in the family. Katrina was the 'other woman' figure, as far as Brenda was concerned, and Brenda was deeply jealous of her beauty and of the place she undoubtedly occupied in her father's life.

Brenda had been with my stepfather as his secretary, since he separated from our mother. She was drawn to powerful men who, like her own father, dominated women by the force of their own personalities. When she was a child her father had exercised what we later discovered was a deeply malign influence on her, as well as on her sister and mother. Her mother committed suicide. On the day of her death Brenda was sent to her mother's room to find out what had happened and then report back to her father who was in the room next door. Brenda never spoke of her mother's death or of whether it was, or was not, accidental. She later fell in love with a brilliant Oxford scientist who ultimately rejected her. Her life's purpose seemed to lie in the service of brilliant men but she did not sit comfortably in the role of servant. She passed over the opportunity to have children because my stepfather did not want them. She was, we later discovered, a talented pianist, and although there was a grand piano in the drawing room, a Bluthner, she never touched it. I think she was afraid of what Dad would do to her if she drew attention to her gift for music.

All of these adult individuals seemed to me like actors vying for the lead part, all of them reaching for a more important role, needing to be noticed, to count as something in Dad's world. Marge was the anchor that held us children and kept us safe from them. She was under the surface, embedded in a deep knowledge of her own that, as I now see it, resonated with God, although she seldom went to church. Her last words to us at night were always "Angels guard you", as well they might.

There were nights when no one else was in the room and the door would seem to open and close again. The latch on the bathroom door would rattle when I was having a bath. Dad would push the door ajar with the words "Coming along nicely. Keep it in the family." It was all a joke, of course. References to my body were a joke too, as were his inferences of how I would feel if he were to have sex with me, or if anyone were to have sex with me. This was what we now call 'grooming'.

It was always after such moments that the urge to remain a child, to retain one's innocence was strongest. I was about twelve at the time of these bathroom intrusions. I wanted to blot out the memory of these moments, to pretend they had not, could not, happen, so with Katrina and the neighbouring children I would play all the harder, all the more loudly. We would run in the sand dunes, run on the beach, or cycle as far as possible before we were missed. We were always running. We would play at 'running away'. I remember looking down at the house on one such morning and making a solemn vow to God. This will never happen to my children. But it was confusing all the same. What was it that I did not want to happen? Had the moment in the bathroom been real or imagined? Would he really have raped me when he got into bed with me on the morning he brought me breakfast on a tray? Was I, in fact, quite attractive to men? So I played both as a child and, I sensed, as this other person who appealed to Dad, desperately joking at the dinner table, as my glass of wine was re-filled for the third time, and then being instantly diminished by the adults at the table in the silence that followed. Our mother would pick up a clever remark, a moment when for once I had felt confident, and reproduce it later, mockingly, saying my name the French way, as if it was royal, but not royal at all, of course.

I still cycled to Mass, in the hope that one day something meaningful would happen to me there. I think that by now I was compelled by something other than the fear of Hell. I sensed the possibility of some kind of connection with God and that the little Catholic church in the village, a converted Nissen hut, could be a home of sorts, a place of safety, despite the fact that nobody ever spoke to me there. There were never any questions about where I lived or who my parents were, but I was grateful for this. I wanted to be left alone.

The Latin also afforded a certain privacy because you didn't need to engage with it. It simply enfolded you like a blanket. The priest was Irish and, to me, wholly unintelligible whether he was speaking Latin or English. But I sensed that for some reason there was a purpose to what he was doing, that it would affect my life in some undefined way and that this, presumably, was also why Catholics were obliged to go to Mass every Sunday, no matter where or how they lived. Cycling back to the house, I tried to connect the Irish priest, the mumbled Latin and the incomprehensible sermon, with the life I really led, wondering what God thought of it all. I failed to make such a connection and I was afraid that the things that were beginning to go on between Dad and myself were my fault, that I was committing a sin for which I did not have a name and that, if I did not have a name for it, I was a liar. I should not even be darkening the door of any church. Very little that went on in the house could be given a name.

Growing up is about naming things. If you experience abuse, especially sexual abuse, you are not permitted to name what is happening to you. You cannot even name it to yourself. You cannot permit yourself that moment of truth, because what would you do with it? So, for as long as the abuse lasts, you don't grow up. It is all a game, a delusion turned into a joke that has no real name. This also makes you nameless to yourself and instils in you a sense of not really existing as a named person, because you are something of a joke. You hate the sound of your name. I dreaded the sound of my own name being called by any of the adults in my life, except Marge who seldom used my actual name but some other diminutive of which I was not so ashamed. This diminutive gave me permission to laugh at myself and to forget, momentarily, the shame I associated with my real name. We learn trust from the moment we are not ashamed to hear our name being called.

Christ makes himself vulnerable in allowing himself to be named by us. He learns trust, in allowing himself to be named by his earthly father and mother, and later by his closest friend. The question he asks Peter is not a test of faith, but a test of friendship. "Who," he asks, "do you say that I am?" (Matt. 16:16) The answer matters to Jesus because it is a human affirmation of who and what he is, in the face of what are probably very human doubts about his own identity and purpose in the life that has been chosen for him. Jesus may himself have felt a momentary sense of awe at hearing Peter's answer, a declaration no less profound for having been spoken by a friend than it was when he heard it from Heaven as he stood in the Jordan river (Matt. 3:17). The name spoken by Peter was, on one level, a declaration of human love, but it was also a divine revelation. It was not a name Jesus was simply known by.[4] The name was the fullness of him as God incarnate, but a vulnerable God who is ready and waiting to be named by us, as he is also ready to be cursed and spat at. In this, he shares in the shame of the abuse victim when the abuse is either denied or belittled because people are afraid to take responsibility for what has happened. Fear, as I was to learn later, makes people defensively angry. From the moment we allow ourselves to be named by Christ, we have our rightful name restored to us. Claiming this rightful name is the basis of faith.

I sensed this despite the shame I felt at hearing Dad speak my name, while alluding to my body in public and at mealtimes. I experienced both outrage and shame at hearing him speak my name in such contexts, at the flagrant denial, and even delight in the pain he was causing, the shame of being undressed in this way. I wanted my rightful name to be restored to me. I wanted to be re-clothed. I sought to experience this re-clothing from other responsible adults,

---

[4] Here, it is worth distinguishing between the Christ as name and other names that Jesus was known by: Son of God, Son of David and Son of Man. 'Son of Man' could have been used in a generic sense, meaning 'ordinary person' or its modern equivalent. When viewed against the background of these other names, Peter's prophetic declaration acquires even greater significance.

from the nuns at school, whose lives I assumed to be modelled on that of Christ but who appeared curiously disconnected from the realities I lived with. They would sometimes question me about my home life, but they did not know what questions to ask or how to frame them. Their questions were more interrogatory than solicitous. My stubborn silence made that inevitable. I felt I was being tested on those rare occasions when I was called in to the headmistress's office to talk about 'things at home'.

Only Marge was at home. Although school was in the Berkshire countryside, I often thought of running away to Marge. There was a trainline visible from our dormitory window and I would imagine how it would be if I could get on one of those trains and then find myself, magically, in Marge's steamy kitchen. I envied the cows grazing in the fields outside the window, imagining what it must be like not to feel this terrible yearning, what it would feel like not to even exist.

It was to Marge's house that I returned the night Dad took me to the Scotch of Saint James, the nightclub to be seen at in the early sixties. I was relishing the thought of telling my friends at school that I had been there in the holidays. The place was crowded. I didn't look fifteen. I looked younger but had piled on the makeup. I think he feared being recognized in this nightclub, which he visited frequently with much older women, but the gins and tonic kept coming all the same. We danced a little too closely. The music was stuff I loved and he would parody it in ways that, in my intoxicated state, made me laugh. I don't know how many hours passed before he took me back to Marge's council flat. He parked in the yard, in his small Mini. There was something absurd about the situation we were in, he being so tall and both of us crammed together in his tiny car. I was later thankful for the fact that the space was so constraining. He could have raped me had we been somewhere more spacious. He frightened me. The rage was just beneath the surface of the unkind laughter, the smell of gin and the iron grip of his hand. I flashed back to that morning when he had brought me breakfast in bed and gripped me in the same way. Abuse events tend to meld with one another. I had threatened to scream. "No one will hear you" he had said, with that same laugh. I think he enjoyed engendering fear more than the possibility of sex. He held me in the car until he was fully in control, then let me out.

I was shaking and speechless when I got to Marge's flat. He had stopped just short of rape. Marge knew instinctively what had happened. "Never mind, lovey," she said, and I understood. You say nothing. Marge never spoke of the abuse and by today's standards she would be judged as complicit, something which she owned many years later; but had she spoken, she would have vanished from our lives. I would often see her strong Scottish jawline quivering with anger and with the frustration she must have experienced at being powerless to say anything.

Perhaps it was in this not saying, and in her grief and anger, that I also learned something of the grief of God. I sensed it in the anguish of our complicit silence. There is something of this anguish in the moment when God appears to turn away from his Son, in that lament of abandonment from the cross "My God, my God, why have you forsaken me?" I felt something of this abandonment and emptiness, as if I was standing on the side-lines observing God's grief secretly, but I did not have a God who I felt I could cry out to in this way.

If, as a survivor of abuse, you have no God to cry out to, you deal with grief secretly and painfully. Grief and shame become two sides of the same coin. Grief becomes 'desolation', derived from the French *desolé*, another word for abandonment. Observing other people's grief is not the same as observing your own. Sometimes, the grief of another person or of whole groups of people, can stir up emotions of empathy, sadness, or outrage, a sadness and outrage that we dare not own in regard to our own grief, still less speak of to others.

In her book *Love's Mysteries*, Rachel Mann asks the question 'who is worthy of grief'?[5] Grief comes with responsibilities of its own. It requires 'response', that someone answer for it, or that you answer for it yourself. So grief is, in some measure, a gift as well as a responsibility. It brings us together, if not with others, then with that part of ourselves that may have been denied to us. A true gift is something that responds to the person who is receiving it. It gives them back more of themselves. Grief breaks us down. It breaks the brittle fears that keep us from meeting others in their own grief and in their fear of abandonment.

A gift is something that enables a person to confront their fear of abandonment. It has that in common with the grief of the abandoned Christ. His abandonment is God's gift to us in the grief we endure in the present moment, or in that which we revisit in our memories. He is in solidarity with us in all this grief, so that we can own it without being ashamed of its cause. We can take responsibility for it. We also have a responsibility for the grief of previous generations, for their silence, whether it is the wounds they carry silently as a result of abuse, or of unresolved, unforgiven hurt brought about through war and the ethic of duty and loyalty to class or country. The freedom we are given to speak about our own

---

[5] Rachel Mann, *Love's Mysteries: The Body, Grief, Precariousness and God* (Norwich: Canterbury Press, 2020) p.3

abuse, the freedom I have to write this book, was not theirs. Marge's silence was as much a product of her working-class upbringing as the silence that was required of me was of mine.

Chapter 3

Flight

'And in the mist of tears I hid from Him, and under running water'

Francis Thompson 'The Hound of Heaven'

My father would visit us in Kent about twice a year. He would arrive with his latest girlfriend who was, typically, a good twenty years younger than he was. There was an awkwardness about these visits. He would try to ease 'the flounder', as we called her, into the eclectic household scenario, she speaking barely a word of English, and he trying to win me with expensive French sweets to which I was indifferent. I would have preferred a packet of lemon sherbets. There was some attempt at conviviality but on the whole I experienced these visits as no more than a mutual performance of familial duty, which ended with my father emptying his pockets of English loose change as he was leaving, which delighted me but infuriated Marge. I was being bought, as far as she was concerned.

He would occasionally visit me at school, but without 'the flounder'. These visits were even more awkward, since there was no third party to distract us from each other. He usually had a hangover, or was slightly drunk. I would cling to his arm, not quite sure of what it was I wanted from him, or what he expected from me. He worried that I might become a nun. Ironically, it was around the time of one of these visits that I had fervently prayed to become a saint, as we were all being encouraged to do. I had no idea what becoming a saint might involve, apart from the smell of incense and candle wax and the scattering of rose petals in processions. It was around the time of the feast of Corpus Christi and I had been chosen to be a strewer, one of the girls privileged to strew rose petals ahead of the Blessed Sacrament in the Corpus Christi procession. Even so, and for all its sentiment, the desire for something like holiness was at the heart of this pristine moment, one that insisted on returning, from time to time as the 'deliberate... majestic...insistent Voice' that Francis Thompson describes in his poem 'The Hound of Heaven'. It was a desire I recoiled from.

Holiness is frequently confused with piety and claustrophobic religion, but truly holy people, in life and in fiction, are seldom 'religious' in the way the word has come to be understood. I think of Graham Green's whisky priest in *The Power and the Glory* and of the women in Patrick White's seminal novel, *Riders in the Chariot.* There are plenty of holy people who would not describe themselves as Christian. They seem to be following a different trail, not an overtly religious one, but one that is lit by its own intrinsic light, enabling the walker to see and love the world, and the most unlovable people, in sincerity and truth.

There is nothing false about truly holy people. They are, like Nathaniel in St. John's gospel, without guile (John 1:47). In other words, they have no need for the kind of power that works itself out through the abuse and manipulation of others. They are at peace with themselves and in every sense complete. The insistent Voice that Thompson is talking about is a kind of constant in such a person's life, more or less embedded in the subconscious, often late to be recognised as a call to holiness. It was a voice I fled from.

There would follow from these pious moments a kind of melding of the spiritual with the inconsistencies of life. Somehow everything was holy and beautiful. Things that went on at home could be 'whited out', at least temporarily, so that I could pretend to boast of a father, if not of a mother. My mother only once came to the school, having just married my second stepfather, Hugh, whose looks combined the best of Clark Gable and the young Sean Connery. I was the envy of everyone in regard to Hugh. My father's image receded. It became a kind of idealisation of what fatherhood was about, something supposedly patterned on the fatherhood of God, although I never really succeeded in making this connection. Since I knew neither of these personages particularly well, I had to construe the idea of fatherhood for myself.

This involved the slow construction of a father I could believe in and would then demand to know. I was, of course, constructing an idol. We invariably demand the impossible from the idols we construct for ourselves. Idols are those things or people in whom we invest not only our beliefs and personal aspirations but whatever it is that we believe life ought to hold for us, in terms of meaning and purpose and of our general becoming. The idol figure must validate the meaning that we are in fact shaping for ourselves and which, as often as not, is the actual destruction or antithesis of the thing we believe we desire. It is a form of 'cruel optimism'.

In the introduction to her book *Cruel Optimism*, Lauren Berlant writes 'A relation of cruel optimism exists when something you desire is actually an obstacle to your flourishing... [It] becomes cruel only when the object that draws your attachment actively impedes the aim that brought you to it initially.'[6] She cites food, love and politics as

---

[6]Lauren Berlant, *Cruel Optimism*, Introduction 'Affect in the Present' (London: Duke University Press, 2011) p.1

examples of the kind of attachments that cruelly defeat their purposes. She could also have cited idealised human relationships, in which one or other party is in a state of 'precarity', a condition of emotional or financial dependency, on the other.[7] My own life, in regard to both my parents, embodied cruel optimism while at the same time creating this climate of precarity in regard to them. I needed to be constantly proving that I was worth the kind of attention I craved from them and what little money they gave me to live on as a drama student in Paris. I fled to Paris soon after leaving school, wanting to re-capture something of the ephemeral happiness of my early childhood and wanting to be French. I wanted to be my father's daughter. I wanted legitimacy, not in terms of the legality of my birth, but in terms of being someone who was meant to be.

My father, willingly or not, had perhaps been prey to cruel optimism himself, trying to be something or, worse, expecting his children to be something, the fruit of whatever he lacked in the way of personal courage. He had been courageous during the war but was entirely without the courage it takes to love your own child more than you love yourself. He was also the product of an age, and of a class, that lived with a sense of entitlement to wealth and unmerited privilege, so he

---

[7] Ibid. p. 192

was vulnerable. He felt shame very keenly and feared humiliation, especially in regard to money and relationships.

He visited the effects of this fear on my half-brother, Philippe, who suffered from depression and, as a result of the way our father treated him, became seriously unwell. Philippe was subjected to the worst and most primitive forms of psychiatric treatment of the time, electric shocks administered in Bellevue Hospital, a state institution in New York. His mother would visit him and find him 'stretched out on a little cot sobbing his heart out, unshaven and thin, repeating that "You and Papa don't love me – I should never have been born and I want to go to God who is the only one who loves me."'[8] Philippe's deteriorating mental health put our father in the position of having to ask for money from his own parents and this was a further humiliation for him. Furthermore, his own education had not prepared him for any kind of profession, but he expected both Philippe and me to 'get jobs and stick to them'. Any talk of university or serious aspirations in regard to a career were dismissed as 'ridiculous'.

Philippe was the child of our father's first marriage to the Bloomingdale's heiress, Grace Cuyler. He was older than I was by many years. I met him when I was about four years

---

[8] Letter from Grace de Mun, Philippe's mother to Albert de Mun, our father. October 28th, 1950

old and did not see him again until after his mother had died. My father forbade any contact with him. When I first met him he had already had his first nervous breakdown. He had already been subjected to the electric shock treatments which destroyed him mentally and emotionally. My father believed that his mental health problems were a game designed to get money out of him and out of other relatives. He believed he was 'playing at it' but all Philippe wanted was to know his father and to have what he called a normal family life. Our father wrote saying he would not 'pay for a lot of psychiatrists' and that if Philippe was 'amused at playing the lunatic, he'll have a taste of a public ward and see if he enjoys it'. He should get a job or enlist in the US army instead of 'disgracing himself and those close to him.'

What did our father fear that made him so angry with us both? Our father did not know what to do about either of us. He did not understand or care about our education unless it brought the kind of results capable of shedding a positive light on him as a parent. As with all narcissists, everything was ultimately about him. It was he who was the victim, rather than those he had harmed and for whom he was responsible.

As a result of the war and of his own upbringing and dysfunctional family relationships, he had mental health issues about which he was in complete denial. He was afraid of anything that did not resonate with his idea of normality. He accused Philippe of being a fraud, of trying to get money out of him by imagining an illness that our father dismissed as entirely 'in his head'. For his son to have any kind of mental health problem was something he could not deal with, just as he could not deal with Joan and K, the psychologists who tried to help me in my earlier years, labelling Joan as a witch and K as a 'quack'.

Our father had no empathy, despite the courage and generosity of spirit he had shown during the war, even to his prison guards. He also had little money. He was a gambler waiting for an inheritance. When he was married to Philippe's mother they had owned race-horses. He had once gambled away the Peugeot building on the corner of the Champs Elysees. He taught me to play backgammon and took me to the races at Longchamps as a child. He also taught me to always honour my gambling debts. But in all this unreality; to be playing backgammon for money when I did not have the price of a metro ticket, to be anticipating Sunday lunch with my father as the only meal of the week (the rest of the time I lived on bread and sugar and late-night leftovers from the restaurant I worked at) made for an unreal existence, a state of mind that questioned the value and purpose of existence itself. I contemplated ending it by jumping into the Seine, but the river was too dark, cold and forbidding and, in any case, I did not want to make a scene in public and make my father even angrier with me than he already was.

It was this drive to legitimise my existence and to find a defining purpose for my life that also drove me away from home, and from my mother, to Paris, in search of an ideal father. He probably did not want to disappoint these expectations, so he created his own ideal in the only way he knew in regard to women. He would tell me that if I was not his daughter I would most certainly be his lover. The difficulty for me lay in trying to hold on to the slender thread of the possibility of some form of loving relationship with him, without allowing it to move beyond the bounds of sexual fantasy. I played to his fantasy from a safe distance. It was the only way to reach him. When he crossed a line, I would run. He would have experienced this running from him as personal rejection, although the lines were so blurred in regard to the way he thought of me that it is hard to know what aspect of him I might have been rejecting. Sexual attraction was the only language he understood in regard to his relationships with women. As I had known no other lines of communication in the context of my relationship with my stepfather, my father and I were as emotionally ignorant of what we were meant to be to each other as two children forced into an unnatural marriage.

But the fact remained that I wanted him to be my father. I wanted to be part of his story but it was not a story that he was able to share with me, although he tried. He took me to the fashionable Travellers Club for lunch, for his friends to admire and later pursue, which he condoned and even encouraged. He wanted me to get to know the right kind of people, people with titles and money. He obliged attendance at balls and parties entirely peopled by the French aristocracy. Otherwise, it was a matter of 'get on the pill, find a job and stay out of my way'.

The hallway to my father's ground floor apartment in fashionable Neuilly had mirrors on either side. They added to the prismatic feel of my life whenever I visited my father, as if my dreams and fantasies, and my own sense of needing to become something were constantly being reflected back to me with the image of myself in the mirrors. Reflection and loneliness and the sheer incomprehensibility of everything surrounded me on both sides of the hallway. On one occasion, after he had slammed the door in my face because I had not warned him I was coming to see him and he had a woman with him, I was very conscious of these endless reflections, of this moment in time and of all the emotions that it embodied, of being endlessly reflected back to myself, as if this was the only way things could ever be.

There was another mirror on the ceiling of my father's bedroom, put there to reflect his sexual prowess back to him, which was conflated in my mind with the mirrors in the hallway, crude sensuality impinging on questions of human worth in one's own eyes and in the eyes of others. Who, among those you loved, mattered enough to make you want to be worthy of them? And what was the price you were prepared to pay for their love? I was constantly drilling for the truth about our relationship, wondering if I was ultimately at fault for not being happy with whatever affection he could show, in between moments of anger and rejection.

Imagery and truth were very mixed. I lived with the images of my parents and of my French family, but rarely saw the truth of them, who they really were as people, until many years later. On looking at photographs of the summer in France, the year our father began to angrily reject and humiliate Philippe because he understood nothing of depression or of what it could lead to if not cared for with compassion and with a father's tenderness (something Philippe had asked for but which had been scorned as an expression of the needs of 'a hysterical little girl') it is quite clear that he comes across as a disturbed and angry man, in complete denial and fear about his own complex mental health issues. Philippe and I, each in our different ways, were drawn down into our father's abyss of loneliness and anger.

We were made to pay for whatever had caused it. This happens with narcissistic parents.

It happened with Polleen, who was quite open about the fact that she had been denied the basics of loving affirmation from her own mother and felt justified in treating her daughters in a similar way. It was payback time. Narcissists treat their victims as scapegoats. The scapegoat figures in the bible as a creature who has the sins of the community ritually heaped upon it and is then driven out of the city to perish in the wilderness. I felt like this when I lived alone in Paris, as if I was paying for my father's unhappiness in regard to his own father and in regard to the fact that he felt angry and guilty about his inability to care for either of his children. He who despised failure more than anything must have known that failing your children is the ultimate failure in life.

At the same time, all the emptiness and loneliness I was experiencing seemed to speak of something. When we are in the very depths of despair, it is only much later that we realise we were not entirely alone. I fled the loneliness by embracing my theatre work and my relationship with the artist, Takis, but more on Takis later.

I also fled the company of one who I sensed, on looking back at these times, was walking alongside me in all this. There is, I have since learned, a measured pace to the way Christ walks with us. He does not flee with us. He walks alongside. He 'roads' with us, as Riddley Walker does in Russell Hoban's apocalyptic novel. He does not rush on ahead chiding us for being slow, but matches our stumbling pace.

I was always either fleeing something, rushing away from something, memories of the past, realities of the present, relationships with men that I could not deal with – I had won them, controlled them but had not what it took to love them. Or else, I was rushing forward in my mind to a brilliant future where I would be successful and famous and triumph over my parents, where I would prove them wrong.

Christ, I later realized, was the reflection in the mirrors in the hallway. He was a wordless presence 'roading' with me, one that I resisted, with whom I could not engage, because of what I sensed of the responsibility that any engagement would entail. I assumed that this responsibility would involve an entirely different way of living, one that would mean a return to the faith I had grown up with but which had ultimately proved hollow and false, a faith that had betrayed its own promise, even though its ritual and the demands it made of me had been a lifeline of sorts.

Meanwhile, other doors closed. I had no qualifications, knew no one in Paris and I had no money. Days were spent keeping warm by walking the streets, reading in the American library, and sitting in churches – Saint Sulpice, Saint Etienne, Saint Gervais, Saint Denis, that magnificent burial place of kings, and Notre Dame. They were, for the most part, warm and there was something about them that assuaged loneliness. I had long ceased to be a Catholic, feeling that the Church and I owed each other nothing. Neither did I need God. I told myself what my father had pointed out, that I was, "Free, white and twenty-one" as if these things were somehow his gift and I owed it to him to make something of my life, just as he expected the same of my wounded brother.

The Nazis and their occupation of France had taught him what it meant not to be politically free and it is perhaps his wartime experiences that coloured his attitudes to his children. We had not seen or experienced what he had seen and experienced. He had twice been a prisoner of war and twice crossed the French Alps into Spain before regaining England and de Gaulle. He had liberated German occupied villages and, on one occasion, subsequently defended a young woman who was being tarred and feathered for having slept with German soldiers because she had a child to support. This treatment of women who were seen as collaborators was common practice in rural France in the aftermath of the war.

My father's relationship with the Church was ambivalent. He had the telephone number of a nearby Catholic priest, as a kind of insurance policy, in case he should suddenly find himself in need of the last rites. Perhaps he believed in something but had no way of giving that belief a shape, or of shaping his own life and its memories to the patterns of religion laid down for him by the Church. This, I believe, is the essence of agnosticism, not that agnostics don't know what to believe, but that the Church lacks the means for making the Christian faith speak to them in the reality of the world we live in and of their own life story.

As Christians, we lack empathy much of the time, and we lack discretion. In the case of the latter, it is as if a person's story needs to be redacted, tidied up, so that it can fit with Christian ideas of forgiveness and redemption. Christianity has not always served trauma survivors well in this respect. It has given the impression that we are obliged to forgive, without allowing the victim to ask why. Often it is the more philosophical religions that are helpful because they have a way of empowering the individual, giving them permission to take control of their feelings. Trauma survivors need to feel in control, so they often redact their memories by shrinking them, reducing them to manageable proportions so that they can be digested and processed over a lifetime, in the way sea birds deal with ingested food by returning it, 'processed', as food for their young. We feed others with the processed or pre-digested food of our own suffering, so that it can sustain and give hope. The pre-digested food is felt in whatever wisdom or empathy we can bring to those for whom we become responsible in any way and for anyone who needs their story to be heard.

The telling and hearing of story is something we have to do for ourselves, even if all we usually succeed in doing is cutting out what disturbs us most. For anyone who has suffered diminishment and trauma in early life, or in a later relationship, this usually consists in trying, often unsuccessfully, to come to terms with the fact that we are loved and honoured unconditionally. The person who has survived trauma in childhood has a deeply ingrained sense of the conditional. There are always conditions that have to be met for receiving the love and validation we so badly need. All of them have to do with conforming to the needs or expectations of a parent, and we are never sure if we have met them or, if we have, of the love that we are supposed to receive in return.

The person who has experienced either mental or physical abuse in childhood senses that the love they need to experience is manifested in their being honoured, or validated, as persons. We honour a child for being uniquely who they are from the moment of their birth. But their uniqueness can put them in direct competition with their selfish or narcissistic parents who are, in their own minds, the only people who must be honoured; that is what maintains them in existence. Others are mere shadows, the backdrop to the narcissist's ongoing entirely self-orientated existence. Narcissists are desperate people, people who are, in a sense, without a soul, or to put it in more prosaic terms, they are people who have lost their sense of self.

My mother, Polleen, had never been allowed to become her own self. Poignant little stories would emerge from her childhood memories, like having a parasol she loved taken from her by my grandmother, on the grounds that it was silly. Such tiny diminishments have a cumulative effect, experienced in one generation and then fed to the next. Polleen experienced much diminishment as the step-child of the eccentric poet, Harry Crosby. She was taken to expensive couturiers where my grandmother would be fitted for the latest fashionable coat or ball dress while her young daughter looked on, badly clothed, poorly shod and with a pitiless haircut. She was sent away to school and left there in the holidays. She lived in her mother's shadow as a non-person. She must have longed to become something, or imagined herself into an identity or persona that would give her the honour she deserved. She was never honoured in the true sense of the word, although she was flattered and later sought after for her looks and her money.

91

Unconditional honouring confers personhood on the other. It also embodies forgiveness and acceptance. The story of the prodigal son gives us some helpful insights into the vital connection that exists between forgiveness and the need for honour. The errant younger son in the story returns home having run through his inheritance and is welcomed unconditionally and honoured by his father. He is returning from a state of non-being, of non-personhood to a relationship of mutual honouring. Paradoxically, it is the other son who is now dishonoured, having chosen to separate himself, to not join in the party to celebrate his brother's re-found personhood. He has become an alienated person. He has devalued his own personhood in a refusal to honour his brother's. Where there is dishonour, alienation follows. Narcissists are people who have been dishonoured at some formative period of their life and now live to recover their honour, no matter at whose expense, but only on their own terms. They can neither ask for nor accept forgiveness, because in their own minds, they are always victims.

In the gospel story of the prodigal son, each of the sons, in their different ways, has chosen alienation at one point in their own story. But the point of the bigger story lies in the Father's choosing to rescue them both by honouring them as sons, beginning with the least deserving, the least honourable, the one who has messed up most, in every sense of the word.

The Father does not wait for the boy to clean himself up. He honours him even though he smells of pigs, is slightly drunk, and has left a trail of destruction behind him; unpaid debts, broken friendships and broken promises. But he is honoured unconditionally.

I think my father understood, in his dying moments, that this is what he had lacked for most of his life. He had never felt honoured in the right way, so he felt disgraced by the children who he believed had failed him, when it was he who had failed us. I think he was deeply conscious of this failure when he asked for my forgiveness as he was dying. I believe he did the same for his first wife, Grace, but I do not know if he did something comparable for Philippe. All I knew of Philippe in his later years, after our father's death, was a broken man, but one who I was told smiled when he received the weekly letters that I began to write to him. I tried to restore his honour by asking his forgiveness on behalf of our father and our father's family.

Children expect to be honoured by their parents. Where parents, or where God, when he is portrayed as a parent, fail them, they look for something or someone else to validate their existence. As a young woman in Paris, desperately seeking a father's honour, I sought this validation through drama school and in my relationship with the Greek artist,

Takis. Acting was all about losing yourself to a situation and re-imagining it from the perspective of the character you were playing while retaining the truth of the situation itself. You could become someone else in experiencing whatever you were being asked to experience on stage and, if you did it well, your real self, the self that craved something like love, could receive at least a measure of approval. Success, to my way of thinking, was the ultimate confirmation of approval.

I craved success. I sat in churches dreaming of success, learning lines that would not only transport me to another situation, as we were being taught to do at drama school, but confer honour. I sensed, while sitting in those churches, that there was some kind of connection to be made between honour and love and that it had to do with God. Perhaps God did indeed square this fragile equation, which I later discovered in the words of Isaiah , 'You are more precious to me than the Assyrians; you are honoured and I love you'(Is. 43:4). But I had already confused the idea of God's honour with fame. Honour, in my partial understanding of it, was a means for shoring up the self that as Catholics we were taught to die to – but how could you die to a self that had been denied to you in the first place? I was confused.

Dying to self had, in my experience, involved a kind of shrinking, the drying up of life and of my own creative potential in the name of a spurious humility, when what is needed, and what is offered in Christ, is something quite different. It has to do with the kind of dying that enlarges a person's capacity for God. I vaguely sensed this as I sat in churches. I did not sense capacity for God as a comforting presence, perhaps because the wisdom and kindness of God held him back from approaching too abruptly such a frightened and lonely person. As a young woman alone in Paris, I had had numerous experiences of men following me in the streets and I was afraid of the approach of strangers, even when sitting in a church. Perhaps God sensed this fear and held back, allowing the idea of honour to remain no more than an idea, one to be considered but which would be rejected as something I was unworthy of, as my father implied in his treatment of me. My father was perhaps right; I was achieving nothing. My life was in small, separate broken pieces; drama school in the evenings, waitressing or simply drifting around Paris by day, or holed up in the tiny attic room I lived in, learning lines for the evening's class.

The waitressing jobs did not last long, on the whole. My thoughts were elsewhere. I would drop a tray of creamy French desserts and idly scoop them back into their pots, straight from the floor, under the horrified gaze of customers. That called for instant dismissal. Night-time restaurant jobs were not much better. I am not an evening person, which didn't bode well for a career in theatre. One of these restaurant jobs had come from a friend of my father's, a contemporary of his who also had sex in mind in regard to where I stood with him. Another of his friends fell seriously in love with me which I found at first flattering and then deeply problematic. At the same time, these older men brought sophistication and something of the validation I craved. I was also permanently hungry and they took me to the most expensive restaurants. My father was flattered by their interest in me which improved my standing with him. He hoped, I think, for serious developments. He wanted me off his hands. He told me to find a lover, which I did.

I met Takis through my grandmother, Caresse, who lived in a Renaissance castle in Italy where I spent long summers, helping her to put together portfolios of the artists and poets she and Harry Crosby had supported or published in the twenties in Paris. I translated the poems of the young Raymond Radiguet. It was the first time in my life I had ever been taken seriously.

Takis worked in kinetic sculpture, kinetic being associated with energy, movement and light. He was twenty years my senior, intelligent, supremely attractive and becoming known in the art world. He believed in his own power and he conferred, if not honour, then at least something of his aura.

He was a means of validation. Just being associated with him in the cafés of Saint Germain, even if ignored by his Greek speaking friends, bestowed an identity of sorts. He knew I needed the validation but he gave it on his own terms, limited to the physical, at times abusive, and to the possible financial and social potential for him that I represented should he decide to marry me. The implied assumption that this proposal would be welcomed was a timely reminder of the fact that my attraction to him, obsessive though it was, was purely physical. He was also another means of assuaging loneliness.

Living as a lodger in an elegant house in Paris, the first of a number of lodgings, I knew loneliness. I knew the loneliness of living on the other side of someone else's walls, conscious of family life going on, of meals being eaten, aware of their polite but not too profound concern about this drama student from a good family who it seemed 'slept around', was out late and took the occasional drugs. I was obsessed with Takis. I lived for those long sensuous phone calls and for time with him, for his validating of me as a person who had a brain, who ought to read more, who might possibly have a life ahead of her with some purpose to it. But he too was a narcissist.

The children of narcissists are often drawn to narcissists. Takis believed he was a primary source of energy, especially sexual energy, and that anything he gave of himself, including his art, was a gift to the human race. But he seemed to have no close friends, apart from his neighbour, Raimondos. Something had hardened in him as a result of what he had seen and experienced in the war, fighting the Nazis in his native Greece. The war had taught him to have need of no one, although he cultivated certain people if they were useful to him. He believed in his own kinetic energy, that his creative energy was generated sexually and from within his own will to life. He believed he was, in a sense, immortal, that his energy would simply transfuse into his sexual partner who would then understand him completely. His energy would endure beyond him in his work which was designed to be in a state of perpetual motion. His work was his religion, but his sculpture, which he claimed was a celebration and embodiment of energy, was strangely cold. It lacked all sensuality and it was without spirit. Steel objects clicked, whirred and blinked. His work left nothing of itself, took you nowhere. I felt the same about him in regard to how he was with me. He left nothing of himself, although he was determined to leave a mark, even a physical one, so that I would never forget him. He said that he would control me for life. There was no tenderness, but that is something I no longer believed I deserved, so I blocked off any desire for it.

With Takis there was always a suggestion of darkness edged with light which both appealed and terrified.

What was strange was his close friendship with Panos Raimondos. Raimondos carved angels out of marble and wood, or from bits of metal left over from one of Takis's sculptures. He was not overtly religious but he understood angels. He seemed to connect with them and there was something oddly angelic about the way he looked, as if he hailed from some other realm. He was small and not very attractive. He was without a partner and had never married. There was something virginal about him. I think he was a kind of protector for Takis and for me too, an angel figure.

Raimondos would come to my grandmother's castle in Italy. I spent the summers there, in order to get away from my mother. The castle had over three hundred rooms. The place breathed heat and resonated with the thrumming of cicadas. The courtyards smelled of yew. The little swimming pool, devoid of chlorine or any kind of filter, was filled in May and left to go green until October when it was emptied, and when my grandmother would move to Rome and Beirut for the winter months. We swam in the green pool, nevertheless. The castle was built in the shape of an eagle with a terrace at one end, the *coda* where I had breakfast above the clouds, watching the buzzards fly upwards and hearing the village church bell ring on a Sunday morning. I experienced a tremendous inner pull each time I heard that bell, but I resisted it. The big *salones* were painted with frescoes that had been covered up during a plague in the seventeenth century. Restoring them became Caresse's life work in her declining years.

Raimondos would help to carry my grandmother, who had a weak heart, in a sedan chair up the hill to the castle entrance. He also constructed an elevator for her. It worked on a counterweight system, the counterweight being exactly proportioned to her own body weight with no allowances made for any possible fluctuation. It was an unpredictable machine. If she had a second helping of pasta at lunch it would refuse to move, but if she skipped dessert it shot, rocket-like, to the ceiling. Sometimes it remained half-way up or down in a state of suspension. There was a small handbell for her to ring when this happened, although ringing it did not guarantee immediate assistance. She could be in the elevator for an hour or more before anyone wondered where she was. Raimondos served her in a proprietorial way, as if owning responsibility for my grandmother and for the situation of which he was a part, and he did the same in a different way for me in Paris.

There was a theatricality to my grandmother's life which I was drawn to. I could not claim any of its glamour, but it helped to be known as Caresse Crosby's granddaughter and it gave me permission to write. It also, I later realised, legitimised a degree of falseness and pretence which was inherent in trying to live from within imagined situations and for a craving need to be noticed, to be attended to. People who have experienced the kind of neglect only narcissists can inflict on their children know about this need to be attended to. The narcissistic parent, especially the mother, has absolute prior needs when it comes to attention. As a daughter, you exist, at best, to serve this need but you are also entirely disposable. You are useful for as long as you make no demands, either practically or emotionally, and insofar as you can service your mother's life, by helping her prepare for the parties she gives and then staying up late to clear them up. The narcissistic mother will find it easier to lavish attention, and sometimes money or gifts, on other people's children. She will fete their successes, praise them for their attributes, for as long as they make no demands on her, which they will never do because she bears no moral or actual responsibility for them and they are as free of any moral obligation to her as she is towards them. She will also be a loyal and generous friend, often to the parents of these other children, making much of their talents and giving them of her time and hospitality.

One of the most subtle and painful forms of abuse that Katrina and I experienced was the demands made on us in regard to our mother's friends. These grew more pronounced as we grew older and better able to service her dinner parties, but never allowed to cook for them. Her friends' needs, practical and emotional, took precedence over ours. Our mother attended to them in ways we never experienced. There were endless house guests at the *finca* she had built in Ibiza, which became home to us from 1961, in the days when Ibiza had yet to be discovered as a popular holiday destination and was known only to a small circle of the fashionable and wealthy, many of them artists. The friends came and went, hanging around in a superficially affectionate way, flattering her but giving back little. Nothing felt entirely truthful or real.

We seemed to be acting out a part in an unreal world. Katrina, Marge and I were interlopers, spectators of something pertaining to the past or perhaps to some greater reality. The view of Ibiza from the house had a pristine quality to it, belonging to some other era. We were imposing something on a people with whom we did not belong. Ibiza in the early sixties was in a kind of existential state of suspension, not sure whether to hold to its traditions and way of life, or sell its soul to tourism. There were no paved roads when Polleen first went there in the fifties, with the current 'stepfather' figure, and just one grass runway for the daily flight from Barcelona to land on. The plane was adapted to local needs. On one of these flights a bull was in the hold below, kicking and bellowing, almost shaking the fragile aircraft out of the sky. Most of the beaches were only accessible by boat. The women still wore traditional dress and the language, *Ibizenco,* was not spoken by foreigners, nor did they try to learn it.

The little white church in the village had a reredos of the Nativity, painted in brilliant reds. The door always stood open, so you could not help but notice its startling colours. I was very drawn to that cool and yet vibrant space. I longed to go in but was afraid of what local people would think if an *extranjera* was to suddenly appear there or turn up on a Sunday morning. I felt a strong pull to simply go in and surrender everything to the Christ of the Nativity. The fragility and the brilliance of the painting somehow spoke into the heat and brilliance of my mother's life, revealing it in all its falsity; the all-night parties that would end on a beach, the drinking, the food cooked by Marge, Polleen's friends, the hedonistic lifestyle we all embraced, and her yacht, which I hated.

Boats have always made me feel claustrophobic and generally anxious. There were those early memories of *Freelander* along with stories of people drowning because of a senseless oversight; lone sailors failing to lower a rope ladder over the side before jumping in for a swim, or intrepid navigators lost at sea perhaps because they had been knocked unconscious by the boom, the heavy horizontal piece of mast rigging that held the mainsail in place.

In all of this, I often returned to the powerful sense of peace that I experienced in the tiny village church and which I found both compelling and frightening. I think this combination of the compelling and the frightening is what people who distrust religion are most afraid of. From talking with people about why I am 'religious', as they perceive it, there seems to be a lurking fear of the idea of surrender which religion does, of course, invite. It invites total surrender.

Before I came to faith myself I feared this surrender and the loss which I sensed would come with it, loss of what was left to me of the autonomy of personhood. If you have experienced trauma or abuse in your early years you cling to what you have left of your own person, if you have anything left to cling to. The age of the individual, which we now live in, obliges us to believe that unless we have complete autonomy, complete control over our lives and the decisions we make, then we are incomplete and vulnerable to being controlled by others. There is a belief that religion, and perhaps Christianity especially, exercises this kind of control, that it suppresses when in fact it does quite the opposite.

The paradox of Christianity lies at the heart of its promise, that you die in order to live and you live knowing that you must die. The dying involves letting go, or surrendering, everything that you have been told you are. If you have experienced the trauma of humiliation or abuse at the hands of a narcissistic parent, you are called to die to the lies you have been fed about yourself and which you have come to believe. You are not called to die to the deeper truth of the person you really are in the eyes of God. The lies you have been fed may even have sustained you in your life up until now, so they are often the hardest things to die to. It can be easier to surrender yourself to the idea that you are ugly, stupid and a disgrace to your father because you suffer from depression, than to find the strength within you to resist the lies and live your life from a different place. But you need to find that strength and, in finding it, discover the truth about the person you are really meant to be. This is what Christ meant when he said 'the truth shall set you free', but it takes a lifetime to learn.

Chapter 4

Becoming

'If anyone is in Christ, there is a new creation: Everything old has passed away; See, everything has become new!'

2 Cor. 5:17

Truth in life is not a theory. It is more like light that shapes meaning out of incoherence and disconnectedness. Images emerge from a dark landscape just before dawn and we begin to see the full picture. The same holds true about our lives. Over time, we see how we are not just the victims of abuse or trauma, but the inheritors of it. We are part of a wider landscape. We inherit the pain experienced by our abusers because they need payback for what happened to them.

When I got married for the first time, to Rafi who I met when he was studying town planning at Columbia University in New York, my mother did not come to my wedding because she was sailing that weekend. Rafi was Palestinian, and later I would come to realise that I had fallen in love with a cause more than with a man. My mother admitted quite candidly that her decision not to come to our wedding, like so many of her deliberately destructive decisions in regard to me, was a conscious one. Her own mother would have behaved in the same way and often did, so this was justifiable payback. I felt betrayed by her and completely alone at that wedding.

Even so, I came to realise that things are rarely as we supposed they were when we look back on them, especially the idea that we are completely alone at any given moment. Perhaps in those moments of aloneness there is someone else who is also alone, an acquaintance, or a relative we barely know because we have never reached out to them. Later, if we take the trouble to meet them, we may come to know them as our companions in loneliness, part of the bigger landscape which is made up of the lives of other people who are connected to us, and beyond them to millions of people who we will never meet but with whom we have something in common.

All moments of aloneness and betrayal are ultimately connected. I think of my brother, Philippe, who lived alone for much of his life, abandoned in a New York apartment as a child during the war, later packed off to boarding schools, then alone in his tiny garret flat in Paris. His loneliness, and the loneliness I experienced at various points in my own life, also join with the loneliness all around me, the loneliness that is integral to the times we live in and to the fears we carry within us.[9] Philippe lived with the trauma of rejection, with the sense that he was utterly worthless in the eyes of those he most wanted to please; our father and our father's family. Although he never spoke, except in an angry monosyllabic affirmation of the deep unhappiness he was enduring in the present moment, I sensed the pain he experienced at having disappointed our father. He lived in a very dark place emotionally but had an innocence about him. His life was a silent protest at their hardness of heart, but there was light in him.

A universal all-encompassing truth about trauma and the loneliness that comes with it hides in the words of the psalmist who writes 'Darkness is not dark to You. The night is as bright as the day' (Ps. 139:11). That is also how memory works. Life experiences are not single events. Those that have formed or distorted a person return again and again, to be re-read and understood by the person one has now become in the *light* of what we have experienced. We learn to see the light through the darkness.

---

[9] See my *In Such Times: Reflections on Living with Fear*, (London: Wipf and Stock [Cascade Books], 2018)

Remembering is not a linear process. It is a re-visiting of experience with the understanding acquired through having lived a life. For those who have experienced trauma this re-visiting can either be a repetition of the trauma itself, or a means of enrichment to others, as well as to themselves. We can choose not to be passive victims. We can take control of our lives by owning the pain and being responsible for how we process the past. So there are choices to be made. As a child looking down at the house where the adults were partying, thinking how vapid and purposeless their lives were, I chose not to re-visit my own trauma on the lives of my children. I wanted them to be free to become fully the persons they were created to be. As a parent, I would later be in a continual state of mental vigilance in regard to how my past must not at any time rebound on them or make them feel responsible for what I might be remembering at any given moment.

For this to be possible I had to learn to live in the light without denying the darkness. Living in the light becomes a means of enrichment to the extent that it makes it possible for us to learn trust, and then shapes how we think and feel in regard to the past. For me, the Christian faith has been vital to this learning process.

Faith is ultimately a very personal and secret thing, at least to begin with. Too many people feel it incumbent on them to talk about their faith, or their idea of God, to go out and 'do mission' long before they have owned their own trauma, pain and the doubts that will inevitably surface as a result of it. If our experience of trauma is to be healing for others, it has to be owned and worked through again and again through the medium of what I would call grace. Grace is the gift that comes with trust in God, but it is often a long time before it makes itself felt. I do not think grace is given to us immediately, from the moment we come to faith, so that we can deal with the pain of the past, and put it behind us. We seem to go on suffering, regardless of faith, or grace, or of the absence of both. My own faltering journey towards faith and healing has taught me one important thing; that in God's economy there is no such thing as wasted suffering, as I said at the beginning of this book.

Many people, especially Christians, cannot look at the trauma they have endured, and the shame of it, because it does not somehow fit with the new person they are told they should be. As Christians, we have been told that we are to think of ourselves as 'a new creation' (2 Cor. 5:17). It is the rich compost of the past that provides the nutrients for a person to truly become a new creation. We are not born again from nothing, but from what has been and from what remains of the pain of the past, either as memory or as an ongoing reality that is lodged deep within us. The task lies in allowing that pain to be converted into something that will enable us to bear fruit, to become the persons we were created to be and always have been.

We become a new creation by allowing, and not by doing. In other words, we have to learn trust. For the person who has experienced physical or emotional abuse, allowing is dangerous. They have 'allowed' too often in the past and their trust has been betrayed. Sometimes this has led to an inability to understand what the idea of trust consists of, that trust is essentially about allowing love, both as something we receive and as something we give in return. If you have been violated in contexts where you expected love and offered it to those around you, you will have lost the instinct needed to give and receive love. It will then take many years for that primal instinct to be rediscovered or, as is more often the case, re-learned.

Religion has been rightly blamed in the past for asking people to see suffering as in some way enriching, but my own experience of abuse has brought me to an understanding about suffering that has to do with how it is quantified in the economy of God, particularly in the economy of a God who we think of as Love. For years I believed that my misspent youth and difficult childhood were a waste, that I had got everything wrong and squandered my life, that it was I who had failed to become the kind of person I assumed I was meant to be, at least in the eyes of God. But in the economy of God nothing is ever completely lost. A life misspent is not a life squandered. It is not a wasted life. It is rich beyond measure in God's eyes, as was the life of the prodigal son. It was the dutiful older brother who had done all the right things, but failed to actually live, whose life was ultimately wasted.

I also like to think of this parable as more open-ended than it is often interpreted to be. There are two sides to the story. There would have been a moment, a fleeting instant perhaps, when the older brother might have experienced something like compassion for his younger sibling. He may have instinctively recoiled from this feeling, but in it he too would have known redemption. He would have known that his own rather colourless life was also deeply valuable to God, although he might not have wanted to recognise this. There is not a single moment in any person's life that is to be thrown away, that is of no value to God.

This being said, there are aspects of our lives which do need to be 'refined' over time. Refinement is about burning away everything that evades the truth, about ourselves and about everything that may have occurred to us in life, so that we can learn to accept ourselves as we truly are. In other words, all that is left of our lives, after this refining process is complete, reflects something of the beauty of God, something of God's image that is imprinted in all of creation and in every human heart.

It follows from this that the healing of memories is a continual refining process, a constant returning to source, a re-examination of events and moments from within that source, in order to effect a transformation, especially the transformation of those habits of mind and heart that have been conditioned by lies. The refining work is the work of grace, that unquantifiable element of God which reveals the goodness and truth that lies hidden in the heart of every person, even if that goodness has been utterly obscured by suffering or by the evil that they may have been caught up in.

Both my parents are part of this process of refinement, insofar as the slow incremental work of grace allows me to understand them a little better over time. To understand is to begin the painful process of forgiveness. Forgiveness is transformative. Understanding, and the forgiveness that comes with it, is not something we do, but something that happens to us through grace. Everything happens by slow degrees in this work of transformation. We are all on a long journey through time, both the living and the dead, abusers and victims travelling together. I think this gives us permission to take liberties with our own stories, given the nature of time itself and what scientists are now able to tell us about it. If we allow ourselves to deconstruct our stories, we can transpose one kind of understanding onto another. We can begin to understand what makes people as they are and we can place them in the wider landscape of their own life contexts, as well as ours.

Take, for example, the story of Christ walking with the two disciples on the road to Emmaus. The event took place after he had died. The two friends had been told that he had been seen by others but they did not recognise him until the moment when, at a shared meal, he broke bread in his customary fashion and shared it with them. This moment of recognition was not a 'bolt from the blue' kind of understanding, or realisation, it was an understanding that began during the course of their conversation. It happened over time, as Jesus was piecing together the various bits of biblical prophecy that pointed to him. Over the next couple of hours, as they walked and then shared a meal together, things began slowly to make sense for his two friends until they finally understood in the most profound way who Jesus was. They had never understood him in this way before. They now had the full picture.

I think this story helps us to arrive at an understanding of how God works in our lives, how things come together over time and become a composite picture. Everything is, in a sense, as it is, because it is meant to be so.

There is a higher purpose, a deeper meaning to our lives, but it is not fate. Everything depends on choice and attitude of heart but we only see this in the moment that we are prepared to trust ourselves and our past into the heart of God. So, in a sense, like the two disciples, we are constantly setting out on a journey, and at the same time always arriving at our destination, our place of understanding, while also permanently travelling. We live with our flashbacks and memories, and with the gut feelings they evoke in regard to our abusers, but we are also travelling forward. It is this thread of continuity, the willingness to see the abuser in their own wider context, and to 'road' with them, which creates a continuity that cuts across time. It will ultimately reveal the graced 'sense' of our lives as they have actually been lived and perhaps, eventually, enable us to forgive.

In my own case, a great deal had to happen, both in my life and in my journey to faith, before I would sense any kind of positive meaning to the false hopes and false starts that had constituted it so far, let alone forgive myself or anyone else. Inevitably, some of these false starts involved other people.

They also involved living in different places, first Paris, then Madrid and then New York. In Paris there were serial relationships. Days and weeks went by, vaguely marked by parties given by the fashionable art set, some of them friends of my grandmother's. There were intelligent risky people there, people I felt instinctively drawn to who were drifting, as I was. The parties reminded me of Ibiza. They were, in a sense, my element, and through them I found something that emulated human affection. They broke up the loneliness too. Affection went by different names in those circles. It had to do with how you looked, how clever you could sound, how youthful and the extent to which your youthfulness lulled men, and some women, into feeling that they were young, at least for the moment. Life seemed to be spiralling away, like smoke. There was little point to anything I was doing or to my being in Paris, since I was not making any headway with my father, so I returned to Madrid. Being with my mother would, I felt, be a bearable price to pay for the home comforts she could provide.

Spain in the sixties was a context in which things were not said. You felt safe in the streets, unlike in Paris, but strangely afraid. The mention of the Guardia Civil to the women who came to help in the house in Ibiza would reduce them to obdurate silence. Spain was a place of constraints. It was oppressively dark and at the same time throbbing with a kind

117

of hidden energy, the energy of its music and dancing in particular, and the natural but often suppressed energy of its people. Its unhappy history and the way that was embodied in the distant and menacing figure of Franco had something of the supernatural about it, and in the sixties, when I was living there, seemed to envelop its life like a kind of shroud. There was a deathly inertia everywhere. The city reminded me of Sundays in London in the early fifties. It was monochrome. Shops sold clothes that bore no resemblance to what you could buy in London or Paris. The city seemed to be suppressing secrets that it was hard to give a name to.

I was compelled by my mother to attend a course for *extranjeros* at Madrid university. Everything was taught in Spanish so most of us understood nothing of what was said, but some of us did pick up on the fear and the secrecy. Doña Cateña taught Spanish literature and history. It was rumoured that she had been imprisoned during the Civil War. There was something urgent and suppressed about the way she spoke. I mentioned it once to a Spanish friend on the bus on the way back from the university which lay on the outskirts of town. My friend went silent. The other passengers froze.

Much of this feeling of oppression and darkness seemed to emanate from the Valle de los Caidos, that inescapable reminder of the Civil War and the monument that Franco built, ostensibly to the fallen, but in fact to himself.[10] We visited it when friends came to stay. My mother, who admired Franco, was in awe of the place. One sensed that it was full of ghosts and it was probably her fascination with the occult that drew her to it. The monument overwhelms the landscape, even from a distance and it overwhelmed me when I visited it, not only with its architectural scale, but with a kind of oppressive darkness. It was always bitterly cold up there on the Sierra, a bitterness that was trapped and compressed in that vast mausoleum, as if the cold had embalmed the bitter memories of the dead. It felt as if the whole of Spain was embalmed there, waiting for its own resurrection. It is said that Franco used forced labour to build his mausoleum and that the five-hundred-foot-high cross which dominates the mountain, into which this vast tomb was built, is seen by many as the arrogant mark of Fascist hubris to this day. In the sixties, a single Franciscan monk was in permanent residence in the church precincts, to be the light in this place of dark memories. Today, there is still a Franciscan monastery in nearby El Escorial. The mausoleum church of the Valle de los Caidos was not like any church I had visited in Paris, or have seen since. If I were to go back there now, I

---

[10] He was buried there. In October 2019 his body was disinterred and reburied in the family vault in Madrid.

would want to claim the light for it, to hold the place and its memories in the light and love of God.

This is no sentimental exercise. Holding darkness and evil in the light and love of God has to be done with one's feet firmly planted in a light place. Every time I visited the Valle de los Caidos I came away knowing that we confront darkness by standing in the light that we already own. The light we own is not generated by positive thinking, although it can be helpful to claim the light through various kinds of spiritual disciplines, especially those that are rooted in religions that have a long-standing tradition of prayer. All people of faith, regardless of their particular religion, ought to be able to meet in these light places. We are all offered the opportunity to learn to pray deeply for ourselves, for the world and, in the context of places like the Valle de los Caidos, for its history. Prayer is not limited to a time-line. But as I also discovered from being in that place and holding its history in my own inner space, my own darkness, prayer is entirely shaped by truth. It is 'validated' by our willingness to look at the truth.

For those who are experiencing trauma or abuse, holding to the light from within a place of darkness is about the determination to hold to something that we know deep within ourselves to be true. Owning and coming to terms with the truth about what happened to us is the beginning of this knowing. It is the beginning of redemption. We hold to this truth by not being afraid to discover why the abuse happened, what made our abuser do the things she or he did. I think the understanding we get from holding to the truth in this way then becomes a gift. So this understanding is not something we work at, but something to be desired. 'Give me understanding that I may live', the psalmist writes (Ps. 119:144). He is not just writing about God, or theology, or any other esoteric area of thought. He is writing about truth in regard to us. He is also asking God for something. For those who have experienced trauma, understanding is given to them as a way of living with the truth about themselves and about all the different ways they have experienced abuse or trauma in their lives. It is not only about arriving at an understanding of how things happened, or even why they happened, although these are both important. The kind of understanding the psalmist is describing is about allowing something like love to take us over, to own us and our memories along with the pain they still cause us. Neither is it about making us feel obliged to love and immediately forgive our abusers. That may take a lifetime. The kind of understanding the psalmist is talking about is God's mysterious love working in and through us now. It is about life. This is what we need to stay focused on. The challenge for us, then, is to trust that this love, or understanding, and the life it brings, is actually happening in *us*.

My own journey from childhood trauma has taught me that we do this trusting through what we call contemplative prayer. Contemplative prayer is essentially about trusting God enough to allow him to contemplate us. It took me a while to realise that I was not being asked to 'focus' exclusively on God in some abstract way, any more than I was being asked to suddenly, and miraculously, 'forgive' my abusers. I was being invited to contemplate him as the person I am, in what Jesus called 'spirit and truth' (John 4:24). For those of us still dealing with our memories of abuse, God is most concerned that we 'understand' in the deepest sense of the word, the length and breadth and depth of his love for *us*. This love is passionate in its desire for justice for *us*. It is wholly devoid of anything manipulative or untruthful. He desires to validate our pain.

I also realised from my visits to the Valle de los Caidos, and from talking to one of the Franciscan monks who lived there, that everyone is called to hold the world's darkness in the kind of contemplative prayer I have just described. All prayer is essential to the peace and stability of the world. There are many different ways to pray in the Christian tradition as well as in other faiths. Whether these are undertaken privately or in community, all prayer that is purposed in love returns us to God who is love itself.

Many people I talk to dismiss the idea of taking prayer seriously, deeming themselves either not capable of it or not 'religious' enough, but this is to misunderstand the nature and purpose of prayer itself, particularly contemplative prayer. Contemplative prayer is available to anyone. It fulfils its most important purpose when undertaken for the good of others. In prayer, we allow ourselves to be 'understood', to be loved, and in so doing we allow anyone who is suffering to be brought into this love, this place of 'understanding', so that they too may 'live'.

When undertaken in this spirit, prayer fulfils a redemptive purpose, so that in allowing this understanding, we enter into God's own redemptive plan for us and for the world. People who have experienced trauma are especially well placed to do this work because they can allow their own pain to be understood as part of a far bigger picture, a far wider context. People who have experienced trauma and abuse are in a position to hold the darkness others are experiencing, so that they can encounter the light in that place. I would add that this particular kind of contemplative prayer is not an exercise to be undertaken lightly, especially if you are suffering from depression or have serious mental health problems, but it does give all of us permission to own our own sadness, loneliness and anger and for these feelings to become transformative in our lives and, ultimately, in the lives of others.

In the monument to the fallen, the Franciscans doing this work of prayer will be claiming the darkness of the past and demanding its transformation. They are engaging in work that we are all called to do, in one way or another, in regard to history and, as I have found, in regard to our own lives. But sometimes there is too much darkness. We experience a kind of claustrophobia, a need to pull ourselves up and out of the dark memories, away from the dark places.

Madrid and Spain were becoming oppressive. Once again, it was a question of flight. So I went to New York with my grandmother, ostensibly to look after her on the journey but in reality to get away from my mother and from what felt like a dark and dead end life with her in Madrid. My grandmother was happy to pay for a one-way ticket to New York, even though I had promised my mother that I would come back.

I stayed in New York at first with my grandmother at the house of an old friend of hers, Mrs Simpson. Mrs Simpson was completely deaf, did not wear a hearing aid and did not lip read, so that all conversations were conducted in writing. She was something of a legend in her own right. Her two ageing Japanese servants had come to her from an American internment camp following the war and had remained with her ever since. There was a note pad and pencil beside every person's plate at the table so that people could communicate with her. There was never the slightest lull in any conversation. She wanted to know everything about everyone and she saw everything there was to see in New York, including the then fashionable musical *O, Calcutta!* which she said she enjoyed greatly. She could sense music without being able to hear it and so was a frequent visitor to the Metropolitan Opera House and the Lincoln Centre for the Performing Arts.

It was at Mrs Simpson's that I also got to know Alexander Kerensky. Kerensky had been head of the Russian provisional government between July and October, 1917, following the Revolution. He was almost blind when I knew him, so I would read him his New York Times at breakfast. Other than that, we rarely spoke, and then only in French. He too had only come for a short visit. He had intended staying for a week and ended taking up residence in the top floor of Mrs. Simpson's elegant brownstone house for more than thirty years.

Mrs. Simpson's house was a kind of home from home in New York. It was also the place from which I married Rafi, again in order to get away from my mother and from the darkness of the past. He was a Jordanian national, as were many Palestinians at the time.

We met while I was working for First National City Bank, Citibank being the trendy place to work. I still had no qualifications, although I had learned to type and my English accent was considered helpful at the time. The hours at the bank were not too long, the work, although boring, was fairly undemanding and in the summer there were weekends on Long Island or upstate Connecticut. Rafi worked for a large architectural company across the road from the bank. He moved in quite different circles to mine. His friends were Palestinian, Lebanese, Syrian and Egyptian. We would sit around for hours smoking as they talked about home, partly in Arabic and partly in English. I had never known such an accepting and relaxed group of people. There was no hidden agenda and no desire to make you feel an outsider or that you were personally responsible for what was happening in the Middle East at the time. There was no rancour between them and me. This was also my first real awakening to politics and, specifically, to the injustices visited on the Palestinian people. But there was nothing violent about Rafi's friends. They were clear about who they were and openly generous in the way they spoke of my own country, despite the legitimate grievances they held against it. They were certainly not terrorists. Later, I would think of them more as zealots, people with a passion for justice, who I would later see as the kind of people Christ chose to be his closest companions. I had been conditioned by the politics vaguely picked up at home, all of them Conservative, with convenient omissions in regard to historical background and much that was assumed and taken to be the right way to think. I was too timid to challenge any of this, and as a result of my patchy education, was without the intellectual wherewithal to do so confidently.

Rafi's friends and his politics challenged all my assumptions, particularly the givens I had grown up with in regard to the assumed goodness of all things British; and hence, in some measure at least, of all things American. As a result, I fell in love with all things Arabic, especially the Palestinian Liberation Organisation (PLO), although my only contribution to it as an activist consisted of sticking the PLO flag emblem onto the insides of subway carriages, going on the occasional demo and joining in loudly when anyone said 'Taesh Falastin' – 'Palestine lives!'. We lived in the not so smart part of the upper East side. Our tiny apartment was dominated by the sounds of the time; *Pink Floyd, Crimson King, The Bee Gees* interspersed with the poetic laments of the Egyptian singer *Oum Kalsoum* and the ballads of *Illa Habibi.* We had an open door policy for all comers. I loved the Arabic language and the Arab people but was defeated by the alphabet. I think I knew at the time that I was marrying a cause and a culture rather than the man himself, but I did not want to face the truth of this or of its longer-term implications for both of our lives. I could not absorb the culture and make it my own, any more than I could absorb the language. Rafi found it hard to love the English who he felt had sold his people down the line. The Balfour Declaration was, for him, an act of betrayal and I sensed that there was something about my own social context that identified me with it. But we were also students together, both of us having started degrees at Columbia University just after we were married, he as a graduate studying town planning and me as an undergraduate majoring in English. It was the first time I had seriously connected with my own intelligence. Lectures, long discussions with other students, discovering Joyce and Chaucer, the intellectual friendships, pretending to be young again. It was oxygen, like emerging from a tunnel into boundless open space. But I was beginning to feel far less like a wife. I wanted to reclaim something owed to me from my youth, but you cannot reclaim bits of your life without someone else paying a price for it. Rafi paid the price.

The marriage was bound to fail. I think we both knew this, but our own friendship endured without a trace of bitterness long after we had separated. The relationship taught me how important it is to be culturally at ease in a marriage and how difficult this is when you try to embrace a culture and language quite different to your own – and do so for all the wrong reasons. While I loved his family, who were always kind to me, I did not fit in with them. The situation was also true in reverse. My family was anything but kind to Rafi. Dad made a point of trying to humiliate him, to which, thankfully, he was largely impervious. My mother did the same in more subtle ways. She would set up situations in which both of us would feel uncomfortable. I would be embarrassed and protective of Rafi at one of my mother's dinner parties and he would embarrass me by refusing to be assimilated into our world. I failed on both fronts. I found it hard to deal with the culture difference in a way that would make Rafi feel at home and I felt guilty about this. It was a challenge to my own integrity as well as to his. You feel someone else's pain in such a situation, more than your own.

I sensed that there was an issue of class as much as of culture in this marriage. Perhaps I had married Rafi to defy the class and culture I had grown up in. Class was something that figured prominently in my early life, along with a degree of culture clash. Life in England was quite different to life in France. Life in our flat in Belgravia was quite different to life in Marge's flat and to the yard where we played with children whose lives were radically different from ours. Each place had its own culture, its own vernacular, and Katrina and I could engage quite easily with both. Language shapes how you think about people. If you speak another person's language fluently, as I did, or if you can slip just as fluently into a regional accent or dialect, you understand not only their thinking but something of their emotional makeup. People reveal themselves most clearly through their primary language, so that if you are bi-lingual, you can know things about people that others may not know. There was much that I did not know about Rafi.

If you are fluent in more than one language, and if you occupy more than one class context, you become two different people. You absorb two histories and become part of them both. A language, spoken fluently, is a context we inhabit and that shapes us, the only exception being in our relationship with God. That relationship transcends all language and all social contexts. At the heart of it is a great silence, a silence that is both safe and yet filled with something ineffable, potentially terrifying, an unnameable greater power that I felt both drawn to and in fear of. I believe we only become fully who we are when we learn to inhabit this place and to be known by this ineffable God. We do not strive to think ourselves into being something that others expect us to be, at least in the context of our encounter with God. We allow God to be fully God for us as we are and as we have been, to be the One. Language, liturgical or otherwise, that has been imposed on us can get in the way, like wearing clothes that are not right for us. The most beautifully crafted liturgy is often too safe. It can permit avoidance. Words create barriers.

For years I prayed in Latin, or rather Latin prayers went on around me. The fact that most of the words were incomprehensible was a source of freedom to simply be in the company of God. The few words I understood still serve as an anchor in the silence when thoughts, memories and preoccupations get in the way of God as he is to be known in the present moment. These words also help me to focus on the suffering that is going on in the world for which there are often no words. So this silence allows me, and millions of other people, to sigh, to pray into the world's need, into confusion, pain and corruption at all levels of life and into all the contexts that divide us; contexts of class, race, religion, sexuality and personhood. All of these contexts are places of belonging within a social order.

There has always been a social order even if it has not always been defined by the same boundaries. The social mores of the world I grew up in, the world of British and French aristocracy, were almost exclusively defined in terms of class. Class coloured my early life but little was ever actually said about it. Today, class has been overlaid by other criteria for belonging, some defined by race and most of them ultimately defined by wealth or the lack of it. Human beings are essentially tribal. There is a great need to belong. Much of what goes on through social media amounts to a cry for company: "Is there anyone out there? Where do I belong?" Our pain seems to erupt all too often into the non-communication effected on social media through angry emojis or cryptic remarks on Twitter.

In all of this, it is becoming increasingly difficult to know if we have reached any kind of destination in our search for whatever it is that we are perhaps really searching for on social media, or through apps that create a kind of safe distance between the user and the real world or other human beings. From what I have heard of people's experiences with on-line dating, the apps allow you to present yourself in the way you would like a potential partner to see you but when you meet the person in question there is often disappointment on both sides. The real person eludes you both and you, perhaps momentarily, elude yourself. The friendship, if there is to be one, will only take you so far. Over time, I have heard, you think the right person will never come along. You may begin to think that this is how your life is meant to be, a series of dead-end encounters and failed relationships, ending with a failed marriage, as I felt when I married Rafi. There were no dating apps at the time, so it was a case of meeting someone who was fun to be with, who would be a complete antidote to the life I had grown used to. It was a case of forcing something to happen that we probably both knew shouldn't happen, in the hope that it would somehow work itself out. Neither of us was asking too much of our marriage. Nothing was real.

There are no easy solutions to how we should be as human beings, to the meaning and purpose of our collective existence, but it is precisely in this place of confusion that we are most likely to encounter God. I found this to be true in the painful early days of my breakup with Rafi, although I was not aware that it was so at the time. A failed marriage can be the worst experience of failure we will ever know. There is a deep sense of things being torn apart in our very selves. Something that was once whole in us, in our mind or heart, has been unevenly broken, even if the marriage was never meant to be in the first place. The failure of a marriage causes an unhealable wound deep within us. I got off lightly with my failed marriage. We did minimal damage to each other, but when I think of the two brief years we had together I am still returned to the question of class and culture and whether it is right to assume that we should expect to be automatically accepted by people who may have reasons to distrust us. This raises questions in regard to forgiveness. If you know that someone is going to be diminished or hurt by your particular historical context, and that there is probably little you can do to either prevent or change this, should you regret having tried to make them a part of it, as I did with Rafi and he with me?

I think this is an especially important question in regard to race today. All of us have a history in regard to this question and most of us wish it were not as it is. But does healing the hurts of the past invariably involve expectations that one or all of us cannot meet immediately? Forgiveness and healing take time. During the second decade of the 21st century right-leaning populist governments gained the ascendancy in Britain, America, Brazil and many other cultures. In this highly polarised political climate, few have the time or the inclination to read the news in depth. But we need something more than one particular viewpoint, based on one set of experiences, to guide us out of the seeming impasse we have reached in regard to race. Where might we find the positive creative energy needed for a new way of thinking about race, as well as about culture and class? How might we meet together in our common humanity? Do we really want to be healed of the fears and hatreds we have all been nursing for generations? I think the way out of this impasse has more to do with things not said and not known, in regard to the other person or group, than to what we do know, or think we know, especially given that disparities exist within ethnic groups and classes themselves. When I did my curacy in a large church in the London borough of Brixton, I was made very aware of the class divides, based on inherited notions of how one or other group behaved socially and made a success of their lives, that exist between West Indians and Nigerians in that neighbourhood. How we think about faith and how we pray matters in all of these respects.

My own physical focal point for prayer is a Coptic Ethiopian icon of the Virgin and Child. I found it in a market in Madrid many years ago, and it lay for many more years at the bottom of a trunk. On coming back to faith I retrieved it and have always used it as my primary 'way in' to God, but it is only relatively recently that I realised that the two main figures are black. Iconography rarely dwells on the specifics of ethnicity, so realising that the figures are black was more than an artistic insight into the way the icon was painted. It was a moment of intense joy and recognition, a homecoming moment. It also embodied the transcendent. In other words, the fact that Mary and the Child are black has now become part of what I am in relation both to God and to my black brothers and sisters, especially those known to me personally. I am 'bound up' with them in God as the figures in the icon are bound up in each other and so draw me into that relationship. They also draw me into a deeper relationship with people of every culture and ethnicity.

This in turn has done much to heal the sense of alienation I experienced as a child. From being someone who was on the peripheries of family life, not belonging in any one context, I find myself, as I contemplate the icon, at the heart of the life of God which is, in many respects, family in its fullest and most consummate form. The Incarnation, the coming of God as son of Mary, gives new life and meaning to whatever our experience of family may have been. It does not change what we remember. It simply integrates itself with our experience without any evasion of the truth. So I can re-visit the pain, as we do when we remember things, but I also know myself to be part of something greater than what I experienced as a child and as a young adult, something which can only be described as ultimate, as purposed. It is purposed, not because God meant it to be that way, but through the way it happened and, by grace and the occasional goodness that came my way, became part of God's redemptive plan, not just for my own life but as part of a far greater plan for the lives of others.

In the case of my own dysfunctional upbringing I see the idea of family, not as something distant and remote from what I experienced in my own family but as bound up in the life of God, held in it to the extent that there is no real separation between the suffering of the past and this 'now' moment, as I travel more deeply into the icon. The same applies to the way the figures in the icon allow me to think about society and all the separations we have created for ourselves as peoples and nations. They make me look at alienation, and even enmity, in a quite different way. The way the figures in the icon are bound up with one another tells me that there is always the possibility of life and creativity, and of belonging, when we make ourselves available to it, no matter what the circumstances. In contemplating this icon, I have a profound sense of the way our destinies, and the destinies of nations and peoples, are bound up with each other. They belong to each other.

Chapter 5

Belonging

'Even the darkness is not dark to you; the night is as bright as the day, for darkness is as light to you'

Psalm 139:12

Belonging, or not belonging, decides a person's life. Remembering or choosing not to remember defines it. What I chose to remember or, more importantly perhaps, chose to forget, about my own early life would shape the rest of it. I chose to forget a great deal. I chose to travel light. Both my parents did the same. They rarely, if ever, spoke of their childhood so it was difficult to know who they really were. They had no real context. My mother hinted at things that 'went on' between her and Harry Crosby and it was only over the years, through making connections and through rare inferences that it became clear to my sister and me that she had been deeply in love with him and he, quite possibly, with her. From what she told us, the only other two men she had truly loved were both killed in the war. She had no real memories of a love that was meaningful to her, that might have changed the way she thought of herself and how she might have lived her life. It seemed to me, from the way she spoke of herself, with a kind of aggressively defensive self-regard, that she did not like herself very much.

Her relationship with Harry may have been the cause of this innate self-loathing. I found a scrap of paper among the many papers and angry letters that Katrina and I had to sort through after she died. On it was a short poem written in French in a childish hand. The child, Polleen, was describing an incident that took place by the mill pond at Ermenonville, re-named by Harry and Caresse the Moulin du Soleil. She wrote simply of small items of clothing being removed, one by one and that she would never return to that pond. I suspect that she carried that memory with her along with a sense of being defenceless in that situation. She was often unaccountably angry. She drank because, she said, she needed the drink as an 'anaesthetic for the pain', something to stop her thinking, to make her not remember.

The only time I ever spoke to my mother about what went on between me and my own stepfather was when she was in hospital after the fall I described earlier in this book. She looked genuinely concerned. Normally, I would have expected her to laugh off the story, to dismiss it out of hand, to tell me that I was being silly, or had been brainwashed. Instead, she asked why I had not told her of this. I replied, of course, that I would not have been believed. She took that as an answer. She knew what it felt like not to be believed. It was also the first time she had ever been genuinely willing to believe me. We finally had something in the way of common experience between us, something that we could perhaps have shared and grown to love one another through, something that we could have both belonged in together. It was the first time either of my parents had let their guard down. She was not, for once, in denial.

Both my parents were in denial about so many things. My father would call me a liar if I dared to suggest that he, or any of his family, had in any way wronged me or my brother. If you are accused of being a liar for long enough by someone close to you your own self understanding becomes blurred. You believe that perhaps you *are* a liar, even though experience may have taught you differently. Eventually you don't know what to believe, so you choose to forget. But memories do not fade so easily. While you may forget the sequence of events, and even some of its details, the weight of them remains. For those who have been abused in any way, they remain as a kind of accusation, that you are a liar and that there is no light or goodness in you. It was easy to get into this place, given the times that I grew up in. There were so many dark secrets then. So little was said about what went on in people's lives. All of this secrecy and silence was further shadowed by the dark memories of two world wars. My parents and stepfather were of a benighted generation. These events alone would have been enough to shatter any sense of goodness they might have had about themselves or the world as a whole. They brought to our childhood a duality, a sense of privilege acquired as a birth right, yet also, in my case, a sense of not belonging, of not being worthy of that privilege, so that I saw myself living in a dark place. Life, for me, as I grew older, was like swimming up from deep water, desperate for air and light, desperate to belong in the light place. Finding the light was literally a matter of life and death.

This is what led me to become a painter, long after my first marriage had ended and I had found life and air in a new relationship. I became a seeker of the goodness, the truth, that lies beneath all created matter as well as in the inner recesses of the human heart. I started going to life drawing classes and discovered that I could draw. Drawing served as the foundation of the colour that would begin to oxygenise my life as an artist. As an artist, I sought to envision the reality that lies beyond things, the reality that we catch sight of from time to time when the light is right and our attention is properly attuned to the transcendent. I only really learned what art is for when I began to do it. I wanted to capture the evanescent goodness that lies at the heart of things, the light that is not overcome by the darkness.

In terms of my own life, and the legacy of the past, art was also a journey of protest, insofar as I was doing it out of a will to resist the darkness that lay within myself and which is perhaps also at the heart of all life, constantly seeking to overpower the light. Those who have experienced abuse, whatever the circumstances or time in their life, will be permanently engaged in this struggle, trying to hold on to the light in moments of flashback or triggered memories. As a painter living with dark memories that I could not share, I sought to dig more deeply into the darkness in order to discover the light at the heart of it.

But I could not simply stop there. I sensed that there was more to this search than painting. There was a purpose to the end product, as well as to the process. I began to realise that painting was a way of praying. In fact it became a contemplative exercise in its own right, almost without my consciously thinking of it in this way. But as with all creative work it was a battlefield. I think, if we are honest about it, all of us who are engaged in a creative process are also engaged in hand-to-hand combat with our alter-ego, that bit of ourselves that needs to be reassured, to be heard, to be loved.

In my case, the battle consisted in not looking ahead to the material results of the end product, whether the painting would make me an acclaimed artist, whether my next exhibition would be a sell-out. But some of the paintings worked. This is something you know as a painter. You know that the painting works, not because it sells but because it speaks to you as if you were in conversation with the memory it evokes, the memory that reminds you of a certain kind of belonging, of the truth of things. When this happens, it happens quite objectively, quite outside the alter-ego. It happens as understanding, the understanding that I spoke of in the last chapter of this book. So I learned that the creative process was not about satisfying the immediate needs of that real and yet quite false persona. I began to understand what I was doing. I was not painting out of a need to express myself. I was trying to grasp, to hold for a moment and then surrender, something of God back to God, hoping that whoever would view the work would receive a little of what I had known in brief moments of profound understanding. I was surrendering this to the viewer, bringing it into the immediate present, trusting that it would in some way speak to their memories, evoke understanding, lighten their darkness.

In this respect, I think the artist who works like this undergoes something of the struggle of Jacob who wrestled with some higher power, with God or with an angel, or with light itself. Irrespective of our memories, or even of the material we are dealing with, we are always working into the 'now' moment, the ongoing actual struggle with light and dark, with our good and bad memories. As with all things that have to do with God, it is the 'now' moment and the struggle that count, because that is where we encounter truth as something experienced, understood, if only briefly, at the deepest level of our being.

Paintings and drawings often require a chemical fixative, a spray to stop the charcoal smudging. The artist who is wrestling with God, and possibly with themselves, is seeking to 'fix' a truth that transforms, or reveals, the underlying life that lies at the heart of all things, to stop it smudging. The person who has experienced abuse may have had their own life and its truth all but smudged out of them by continual rejection, something which they may also have subconsciously set themselves up for. They failed to allow the truth about themselves and about their gifts, with all its dangerous life-affirming possibilities, to become 'fixed'; perhaps because they were afraid of what would happen if they did.

If you believe you are not worth anything, you set yourself up for being dismissed as worthless, for being thought a liar.

You take the path of least resistance out of laziness and out of fear. You fear what you may have been in denial about for years, so you give up on yourself. Or you become a narcissistic parent or partner, one who seeks the destruction of another's creativity or gift for life for fear of what it may do to you, that it may destroy you. Fear makes the narcissist envious.

I sensed this envy, and the fear, in regard to my mother and her attitude to my painting. Envy wants to destroy what another person is or does. Jealousy simply wants to possess it. The envy of a narcissistic mother seeks to destroy by undermining the very foundations of her daughter's sense of selfhood so, as with the attention she paid to other people's children, my mother would make a point of noticing and sometimes buying other people's work. I found this deeply wounding. As a Christian I tried to tell myself that I should think of it as an opportunity to be more humble. A great deal of nonsense is talked about the Christian virtues, especially that of humility.

I felt more sorry for my mother in regard to her attitude to my work than I did for myself. I had had two exhibitions and my work had sold well. Her deliberate rejection of it revealed something of herself which diminished her, and which I think other people noticed, and it made me ashamed for her. I think her behaviour in regard to my painting was also an expression of anger that her own gifts had been stifled. She could write well. She had wanted to study law but lack of encouragement, too much money and too many distractions had sapped her of the will to pursue anything outside the gratification of the narcissist's immediate needs for personal affirmation. She knew that she could not reach or control me through my work. There was also no possible line of conversation open to us in that context because she could not, or did not want to, understand it. Added to this was the fact that the way I painted was part of an exploration and journey of faith and she had no time for faith. She believed God was 'out there' in a kind of cosmic way. She mistrusted an official religion which she assumed that both Katrina and I, each in our different ways, had either bought into, or that we had been simply 'brainwashed'.

She had a point. There are different ways of surrendering when it comes to faith. There is passive surrendering in which a person surrenders emotionally and is often vulnerable to being manipulated or abused by charismatic church leaders. But there is also active surrendering, a conscious decision to bring everything a person has, both intellectually and emotionally, into the light of God. Passive surrendering is both dangerous and ultimately fruitless. It leads nowhere. It disempowers and can wreak immense psychological damage

147

on individuals as well as on whole groups of people, both in a religious and secular context. Active surrendering is about desiring to understand, to learn, to 'make sense' of mystery, which is an oxymoron in itself, but one which is life-giving and inherently dynamic. A person who is 'making sense' of mystery is on a journey, always moving forward but always mindful of what lies behind them, of the realities of the present moment and the present set of circumstances. In other words, they live in a kind of eternal constant, in the 'now' and the 'not yet', when it comes to the meaning and purpose of life as we understand it. They are always being drawn 'further up and further in', to quote C.S. Lewis, who concludes his Narnia epic with those words.

Not long after I left for New York, ostensibly to look after my grandmother, Katrina went to Oxford to read medicine, and then to Nepal where she spent six months on placement working with leprosy patients at the Shining Hospital in Pokhara. There she met Angela who was an Australian doctor and a charismatic Evangelical. She introduced Katrina to an Evangelical expression of the Christian faith. Angela's house was built on stilts, to protect it from flooding and from being invaded by the colony of snakes that lived underneath it. Katrina shared my horror of these creatures, so having them around at such close proximity must have tested her new-found Evangelical spirituality to the extreme. She returned to

England full of peace and with an inner strength that had grown softer, tempered by having encountered the love of God. She and her husband were two of the first people to become part of the burgeoning Evangelical charismatic revival in the early 1980's and of Holy Trinity Brompton (HTB), which they saw grow from a moderate sized Anglican church, slightly in the shadow of the Catholic Oratory next door to it, to the HTB that would launch the universally acclaimed Alpha programme. She had found healing there, but without the trappings of Catholicism. She had wanted to become a Catholic while still at school but had been prevented from being baptised by our mother. Now, she was able to absorb and benefit from Evangelicalism. My problem with Evangelicalism was largely a matter of never having felt completely at home with Protestantism. The lack of sacramental focus rendered Evangelical worship meaningless to me. It lacked mystery.

There were doctrinal differences too, where Evangelical churches were concerned, especially in regard to the primacy of scripture and to the way it was taught. As a Catholic, I seldom read the Old Testament. It was treated by the nuns at school as a collection of 'jolly good stories' interspersed with some beautiful poetry, some of which got incorporated into Catholic liturgy, although always in Latin. The liturgy left me with a feeling for the cadence of scripture before I understood and learned to love the words. I think this sense of the innate rhythm of the psalms especially, and of the Wisdom literature in the Old Testament, can provide a kind of subconscious nurturing for the soul and perhaps prepare us for what will be required of us if we embrace the kind of prayer that relies on only very few words.

I went along with Katrina's new experience of Christianity, trying to re-connect with God in the way she seemed to be doing, but I had a problem. I did not trust organised religion that preached what seemed to me to be a gospel of guilt and retribution. I also sensed personal judgment, something that I was already living with as a legacy of how my parents had taught me to think of myself, and of my earlier life as a Catholic. It seemed that if you became an Evangelical, you had to conform to and comply with a set of rules and expectations in order to be eligible for the kind of salvation being preached at HTB. You could be a Catholic, perhaps, but this did not mean that you were a Christian. Catholics were tolerated in a patronising way, but I sensed that it would have been impossible to remain a Catholic and be part of HTB and the Evangelical revival movement. The Catholic Oratory across the road had something I still yearned for, but it was associated with dark memories and with a religion that was distant, incomprehensible and, in terms of the salvation it offered, as conditional as that being offered by any Protestant church. Evangelicalism was, in a different way, just as alienating as Catholicism. I also sensed that there were categories of people who were not fully accepted, who did not really qualify as Christians because of their sexual orientation. There was something deeply hurtful about the trope 'loving the sinner but hating the sin' and the way it was unquestioningly quoted and accepted. How, I wondered, could you really love a person if you judged their very personhood as inherently sinful, as 'tainted' in some way because certain passages of scripture, read out of context, said they were? At the same time, my Catholic conscience made it difficult for me to question the inerrancy of scripture; I had previously been taught not to question the inerrancy of the Church's teaching. The way the Old Testament and parts of St. Paul's writing were being taught at HTB triggered old memories of fear, unquestioning subservience to religious authority and general guilt in regard to God, faith and the Church.

I began to realise that I had also had enough of guilt and general unworthiness as a Catholic and simply could not buy into it again. I felt confused and disorientated in regard to faith as I was now trying to experience it. If I was going to join an official branch of the Christian religion, I needed somewhere that would offer unconditional intellectual, artistic and spiritual hospitality, a place where conversation was valued. I found this eventually in the context of Anglicanism.

The idea of the Anglican Communion as an inter-related body of autonomous churches is, or ought to provide, the ideal setting for ongoing dialogue, for a continual process of learning across the barriers of denominational difference, or so it seemed to me at the time. But Anglicanism is also all too human. Fear of the other ultimately distorts its message, as old fears and prejudices creep back into its life. Churches are made up of human beings and human beings like to conform to a pattern they think they understand. This leaves very little mental or emotional space for genuine dialogue, the kind of dialogue through which we re-learn how to love one another, across our differences, confronting our fears together from within the depth of God's own love for humanity. We must always be judging one another and, more often than not, condemning those who we don't understand because they are 'not like us'. In the Church, as elsewhere, we find genuine conversation difficult. We find it hard to surrender the preconceptions and 'givens' that we have been wedded to for centuries, be they sexual, racial or power-related. All of this compromises our mission, our conversation with other faiths and with the secular world. Mission begins and ends with genuine conversation, conversation that takes place between people at the deepest level. Genuine conversation requires trust.

We cannot have genuine conversation without being essentially true to who and what we are. For those who have experienced abuse, this can be difficult. We have been fed so many lies. We do not always know who we are. If we do, we are afraid of what people will think of us, even those who are close to us. But in belonging in and to Christ we do know that we are a person who is known by God and belongs to him. For those who have experienced trauma and abuse in early life, it can take them the rest of their lives to come to terms with this. Sometimes it is easier to deny this belonging altogether and, as I found, to simply carry on believing the lies. We can deny who we are and simply coast through life hiding behind the person we have come to believe we are. As a result of this hiding, we can become detached from those who are closest to us and who expect the most of us. I think this is what happened to my mother. Deep down she did not like herself or believe in the person she was trying to project, especially in regard to us as her daughters. But I also sensed a kind of conflict at work in her. At times, often surprisingly, a genuine moment of tenderness would emerge, when we were ill or frightened. One of these occurred when I was eight. I had overheard her discussing money with my grandmother. I had never thought about money very much, despite Marge's efforts at trying to give us some awareness of what having it, or not having it, could entail. My mother found me crying because I was afraid that when I grew up I would not be able to pay my bills. There was, of course, no suggestion of making a career that would enable me to pay them. But there was a moment of genuine concern, even if her ignorance of the real world gave me permission to retreat back to a place of denial of any kind of responsibility to myself in regard to making a living. I was conditioned to believe that life expected nothing of me, that I had nothing to give and to assume that one day a husband would materialise who would take care of everything and support me financially. There were no meaningful goals or responsibilities to hold to.

It is only when you experience the imperative to love that you 'wake up' to responsibility. If you have not known love at the hands of your parents, you will wake up to it when you become a parent yourself, as I found, years later, when my children were born. Not all survivors of abuse are able to do this. They are too wounded and angry to be vulnerable to the kind of love that takes a person over when they become a parent. They simply cannot risk the pain of getting it wrong in regard to their own children, so many abuse survivors remain outwardly cold in this respect, often repressing their deep love for their children, or at least making it invisible. They have a very thin shell which, if it were to be broken by forces beyond their control could prove catastrophic, not only for them but for the people they love.

Children have no preconceptions about their parents, although they will have expectations. They will not be making allowances for anything their parents may have endured in their own childhood, because they will not know about it, unless the parent chooses to tell them. They will need and expect a parent to be a parent to them, regardless of that person's history, as they have the right to do.

They may even tell themselves that this is what is happening, when it clearly is not. I would lull myself to sleep at school by imagining I had perfect parents and a perfect life at home. I think that when parents wilfully ignore this need to be loved unconditionally, and deny it to their children, they live with the consequences of their denial for the remainder of their lives. My mother lived with a deep-down sense of guilt and failure. One sensed that she drank as a way of hiding from the reality of having denied her children the kind of parenting she never had and from the pain that denial caused her. She drank to hide that reality from others as well as from herself. Children ground you in reality, so if you deny them the unconditional, uncritical love they need and deserve, you yourself become a casualty of that denial. You become an alienated individual, someone who has no sense of ever having been grounded by belonging to someone else who loves you unconditionally. If you are not grounded in this way in early life, you cannot adapt and learn to live with others. You never learn to love, or to receive love, so you belong in the end to no one. You will also find it hard to be a parent. The abuse syndrome repeats itself down through the generations. My mother had never experienced the grounding she needed in order to love and parent her children. Katrina and I had our grounding from Marge. It was Marge who supplied the pattern for us to live by in the context of rearing our own families. Katrina adhered to it perfectly. I failed often. I made some wrong choices.

There are, for abuse sufferers, times when they must make choices. They must choose whether to give in to a pattern of behaviour that they may have learned from parents or people close to them, or whether they will refuse it. Abused people will not invariably become abusers themselves, as is often supposed, but they may occasionally slip into that pattern without realising it at the time. They can choose not to revisit their suffering on others, especially on future generations, but it needs to be a deliberate conscious choice, consciously adhered to, always remembering what it was like when you were growing up, but never speaking of it, never imposing it on the next generation. This is not just a matter of not becoming an abusive parent. Neither does it amount to making the best of things by choosing to 'forget', as my generation was encouraged to do. It is somewhere in between. Today we are encouraged to remember, and then re-work our lives from a place of honesty, knowing the pain for what it is but also learning the trust needed in order to be open to the possibility of actual happiness, which means belonging to our immediate human community and making it possible for our children to acquire this sense of belonging. We try to help them learn how to be happy.

For the trauma or abuse victim, the possibility of happiness can feel disturbing. For one thing, they have been conditioned to quite the opposite of happiness. They are conditioned to not belonging. They therefore have no right to the kind of happiness that comes with mattering to someone. The shame they have known conditions them to being an outsider, to a state of permanent alienation in the way they think about themselves. They become alienated individuals who know pain and have grown used to it. Suffering may even be a kind of safe refuge. They do not want to adapt to something new which is quite outside their emotional frame of reference, their psychological 'comfort zone'. Perhaps it is the fact that the person who has experienced trauma or abuse is dealing with something that is already theirs, but about which they are in denial, that makes surrendering fully to it so difficult and disturbing.

What we are dealing with here is the pull from God, a tidal pull that draws us to itself even as it returns us to the shore of stability and human happiness. So nothing changes and yet everything changes. We belong to our past, but we do not embody it. Our memories remain what they are. We must remain true to them, but we must also be open to the possibility of things changing, despite the acute pain that can at times overtake us. We still need to do the re-visiting when our memories press upon us, when they demand that we own them as true.

Pretending that life was, or is, any different from the truth leaves us burdened with a lie that ends up being too heavy to carry. It ends, quite literally, in breakdown. So it is important to get help, both from outside, through competent practitioners, as well as from within. Ideally, the victim of abuse should be given the chance to access both kinds of help, but where this is not possible, it becomes essential that they should learn where to find what they need in order not only to survive, but to fully live their life from their own inner space. This is the space where life changing graced encounters take place.

Chapter 6

Encounter

'Who touched me?'

Luke 8:45

If you have experienced trauma in childhood you may spend the rest of your life trying to erase all the negative connections that contributed to the abuse, in order to minimise the pain you experience in the present moment, but in doing so you risk confusing, or even losing, the story. You will not be able to recall exactly where the pain began, or where surprising moments of unadulterated joy took over. These are graced moments that have the power to heal, no matter where they occur in a person's life. They heal because they work themselves into the pain, perhaps before it has even occurred and, if we allow them to, later, when we return to them in our memories. When I think of these random moments of unaccountable joy I begin to see God's salvation at work.

I am taken back to summer mornings on the beach, being released from the house, the first deep intake of boisterous sea air, the rush of light, the pressure of foot on pedal, pushing and pushing, away and into the essential goodness of the moment. I think of moments of graced intelligence, of when my own intelligence was momentarily revealed to me and I could own it. The grownups were wondering about a crossword puzzle clue 'the energy of the male cat'. The answer was obvious. They were surprised and a little annoyed that I instinctively came up with it. "Are we harbouring genius then?" Dad asked. It was good to be noticed, to be valued, even in passing. It was more than a salve to the ego. It was a salve to the soul. I would surreptitiously fill in bits of my mother's or Brenda's attempts at the Daily Mail crossword puzzle. They could never understand how these infills got there, and how the puzzle then solved itself. I remember the sinful sweetness of candyfloss, paid for by Marge out of her own wages, the first intoxicating bite. Such outings were graced events. I could forget what was going on at home for a while. Marge's goodness was the healing agent.

Later, comes the memory of another beach, and of being in love with Fernando, an artist who I had met in Paris. 'Cala Llonga' was then a small sandy cove on the undiscovered island of Ibiza. There had been supper with friends and we all went there long after midnight under a full moon to swim in the phosphorescent sea. The freedom, the untrammelled, uncomplicated joy of the moment and then returning to the finca of another artist, to finish the night with tiny glasses of *hierbas* and having one's portrait drawn by him. It was good to feel beautiful and to feel so loved. For a moment I was not a liar, to myself or to anyone else. There was nothing tainted or duplicitous about any of these encounters. The joy lay in the freedom and in being wholly accepted as I was, that I was not fundamentally a liar and a fraud. Grace was at work in me without my knowing it.

For the abuse victim, being made out to be a liar, or not being taken seriously, can inflict a deeper and longer lasting wound than the moment of sexual abuse itself. It may be that people accuse you of lying because they are afraid of you and of what you represent as a reminder of something that happened in the past, something that they would prefer to ignore or forget. You therefore have a certain power over them. But you may also experience the profound release, and the joy that goes with it, in knowing that you do not want power over another person, especially the power to hit back or take any kind of revenge (possibly on an unrelated third party) for what you have experienced. You will have acquired, through grace, the peace which comes with understanding what makes the abuser behave as they do. Nothing more is asked of you, because to understand is to forgive. In the forgiveness that comes with understanding, you will realise the extent to which fear has dominated not only your own life, but very often the lives of your abusers as well.

My own story is heavily conditioned by a combination of not being taken seriously and, I now realise, of other people's fear. It was important that I conformed to a particular version of myself, so that everyone else could feel safe. A neutral, not too intelligent or articulate version of who I was seemed to pose the least threat. I was happy to go along with this because it also allowed me to ignore my own shame about who I really was, as opposed to the person I was trying to be and believed I should be.

Shame is something we experience not only as a result of coming to terms with the truth about something that is done to us, but as the result of being made into a person that we know is not who we really are. In my own case, I experienced shame in being this false person. The moments of healing grace, and the joy that came with them, allowed me a glimpse of the person I was capable of being, both intellectually and in terms of my relationships.

Abuse begins in the conditioning of one's self understanding, that you are not really deserving of protection because you are not beautiful, clever, or simply a *bona fide* member of the family group. Therefore, the sexual abuse is permissible and, more importantly perhaps, no one is under any obligation to take responsibility for you because, strictly speaking, you are not their problem. What this emotional neglect does to you is not their problem either. Your task, then, is to break down the protective barriers that you have either put up for yourself, or allowed those who were either directly or indirectly responsible for the abuse, to erect for you, in order to contain you in such a way that you pose no threat to them. My own relationship with my mother was defined by these parameters.

The barriers we put up for ourselves, in an abuse context, are what we hide behind. The barriers others put up around us are what they, and our abusers, use to hide us from them. In families like mine, where secrecy prevailed well into our adult lives, we lived in separate, isolated emotional environments in regard to one another and we remained for the most part in denial about this.

At the same time, abuse and trauma victims are not entirely helpless. We still have a measure of control over how we will shape our life in the future. We know that one day we will have a choice. That day is not in the remote future. It is right now in the present moment. So right now, in the present moment of depression and general hopelessness, if that is what you are experiencing, you have work to do that will determine whether you actually decide to live or not. It is knowing that there is work to be done, not only for oneself, but for fellow survivors, that motivates us in the darkest moments to actually get out of bed in the morning. For many who have only just survived extreme forms of violent sexual abuse, even that choice can be a life-deciding one. But once you are up and out of bed you have opted to stay alive.

Sometimes the decision to live will be forced on you much later in life, when the memories you thought you had buried resurface. I discovered this shortly after my separation from Rafi. The divorce itself was not all that traumatising, but the process of separation acted as a trigger. It took me back to the place where I was not sure whether my life was, or ever had been, worth living, or whether I deserved to live at all. I had run out of ideas when it came to persuading myself that there was something to live for, so I reached for the half bottle of paracetamol that was in the back of the bathroom cabinet. The few remaining pills that I swallowed would not have killed me, and I think I knew this. It was meant as a cry for help and attention, a gesture designed to frighten people into taking notice. I got no help and the only bit of attention I received came in the form of a telegram from my mother telling me to 'cheer up darling'. Under these circumstances, you soldier on, patching up your wounds as best you can with whatever means lie at your disposal. One option that was not open to me, I realised, was alcohol. I would not become an alcoholic. I did not want to be like my parents. Drugs were a possible alternative, but they seemed to be only a slower, messier and more expensive way to do what I had tried to do with the paracetamol. So there seemed little left other than to get a grip on life as it was and try to turn myself around. I wanted to find a thread or connection that would help me do this, something that would help me tie my life together so that the past might eventually reveal some kind of purpose and sense of connectedness, that I might not be entirely alone in it. I needed to trace the connections that would help me to remember my life differently. I needed to connect once more with those moments of joy, some of which did not always fit with my memories of the people involved. But they did oblige me to see these people in a different light, to remember them fully as they were.

My complex relationship with my mother played an important part in this process. We would often find ourselves in ludicrous, almost burlesque situations, as on one night in Montparnasse when we were caught up in the celebrations of a local football team. My mother had, in a moment of rare maternal concern, come to Paris to help me sort through my father's things. We went to a café where an entirely masculine crowd took us to itself as if we had been part of the scene from the beginning. We were hysterical with laughter.

This is something that often happened in our relationship. She had a sense of the absurd and used her excellent knowledge of French to perfection when it came to seeing the funny side of things. Speaking French created a particular bond between us, but she could also use the language we shared to torment me with, choosing exactly the words needed to humiliate and control, knowing that only she and I understood their full meaning. That is what made the relationship so painful. When you experience joy with someone, you trust them. Laughter always establishes a connection, or deepens an existing one.

Part of the process of living involves retracing our steps, revisiting those moments when a connection was made and, perhaps, where trust was broken. In doing so we may discover other moments we had never noticed before, like the one in the café in Montparnasse which I am only fully remembering as I write about it. These are the missing connections in our lives which fill out the picture. They are especially important in the context of abusive relationships. In more general contexts they serve to give a life its substance and meaning. They are not always remembered as vividly as the one I have just described. They may consist of events that might have happened, but did not, in words that were perhaps spoken but of which we were either unaware, or else did not understand or listen to at the time, or in words that were never spoken at all, but might have been thought. These comprise much of our half- remembered childhood memories, things we wish we had said or done, like challenging the behaviour of adults in ways that today would have won us a hearing but in the fifties and sixties, and in the social class I inhabited, were not permissible. Katrina and I were brought up to believe that children should be seen and not heard. I hated being seen because I believed I was ugly, so it made the trope all the more painful to hear. It is in all these unspoken, undiscovered connections, and the emotions they trigger, that the pain we might have endured re-surfaces. It is remembered for what it was, or continues to be, by virtue of the story being told. The connections matter, along with the relationships they influence. So the events and memories I have described in this book are connected in ways that allow these stories to be told 'slantwise', coming at the truth from different perspectives, in the light of experiences past and present. The truth of a memory encompasses more than the event or conversation itself. It is also made true in the telling and, most importantly, in the hearing and believing. The way stories are told and read can also change them, in the way a particle examined under a microscope is changed by the examination itself. The event itself may have become a 'touch point' in a person's life – if it is consciously remembered – so the memory of the event can bring other memories to life, for better or for worse. I have written this book in order to allow people to do the same thing with their memories, especially those they associate with abuse or trauma, to allow the 'touch points' to surface so that grace can be worked into them.

Trauma survivors will have tried from time to time to erase the past, or certain 'touch points', in an effort to forget, with the result that what is factually true becomes blurred with what might have happened if things had been worse. We sometimes do this by placing whatever did happen in a larger landscape of something worse that might have happened, in order to make what did happen feel less significant and ultimately easier to dismiss to ourselves as imagined or untrue.

My experience of near rape with my stepfather was one such moment, as was the occasion when my own father assaulted me sexually. I remember the moment. We were arriving at the house of some friends of his and I was about to press the doorbell. I experienced a visceral fear as he momentarily lunged towards me. It was not going to be an affectionate paternal hug, but there was also confusion in it. He wanted to be a father, but he only understood women in terms of their sexual potential. That is how he gauged their worth and it is how he gauged mine. It was the only way he knew. But the moment passed quickly. He had sensed my fear as he was about to grab me. We had both pulled back just in time. We had supper with the friends whose doorbell I'd rung and talked about their children and whether or not I had taken any 'O' levels, as GCSEs were then called.

I tried to absorb the incident into the repertoire of sexual innuendos he would level at me on a regular basis, and so normalise it, but it remained deeply embedded as a memory. He had tried to touch me in a way that felt dangerous. The memories of trauma that endure are invariably those that touch us, both metaphorically and physically. Nothing can live without having been touched in some way. We live by touch because we live in and through our relationships, our connectedness with others.

I think this is true of our spiritual development as well. From the moment of our birth, we develop through touch, even if the touch is not physical, but something sensed or intuited as love. But we do not always develop in a linear or incremental way. This is where telling the story of a journey that is essentially spiritual becomes difficult, because the expectation is that a story will be incremental, that it will build on itself as it moves in a forward direction, from beginning to end, but it is the connections that weave it together that give a shape to the story. The connections that embody love will underpin and rebuild the ruined places in a person's life story. Some will trigger pain. So we have to revisit our memories accurately and try to see them as part of a bigger picture, if we are to reclaim our lives, and our proper selves. But it is hard for a person who has experienced trauma in early life to remember the various pieces and put them together so that they form a composite picture. How do you reclaim your true self from these 'scattered shards', as Susan Brison describes them?[11] Trauma and abuse scatter the self into shards. The survivors of major trauma experiences may spend the rest of their lives trying to either return to the place they were in before the event happened, or else come to terms with the different shattered person they have been reduced to and try to begin their lives from there.

Neither of these options are open to them because trauma requires that you compress your past in such a way as to create a kind of clean slate. You erase things from your memory but you do not 'forget' them, even though you may have taught yourself to doubt them. As a result, it becomes impossible to create a meaningful continuous narrative about one's life without being beset by doubts, not only about the truth of the narrative but about the trauma-triggers and incidents of abuse themselves. The events have been 'rubbed

---

[11] Susan J. Brison, *Aftermath: Violence and the Remaking of a Self*, (Princeton University Press, 2002)

out' like chalk on a blackboard. How can I know they really happened? But if they did not happen, why is there this vortex of nothingness when it comes to remembering the past?

In all of these questions, ideas of 'getting over things' are entirely mis-placed, even if well meant. Still more mis-placed, for Christians, is the notion that somehow God is 'using' the experience to make you into a stronger better person, someone who is particularly graced by suffering. Many years have elapsed since my own trauma experiences and over the span of these years I have learned something about the activity of grace. Grace does not 'heal' you in the way many Christians think of healing. Rather, it enables you to live truthfully from within those wounded places, even when echoes of the childhood trauma are all around you. Living truthfully requires acute, sharp-edged memory.

It is important if you are to be a source of grace to others to learn how to remember acutely, as well as accurately. In other words, we must learn how to remember and, when necessary for the good of someone else, relive the pain itself. It is also important not to suppress triggers. In other words, where pain recurs, or is re-inflicted by an old abuse, it is better to go with it without allowing it, and the associations it brings, to overwhelm us emotionally. We need to go on experiencing these moments of acute pain so that we can be with others when they tell us of their own experiences.

I think of a moment I experienced with my narcissistic mother, much later in my life. We were in a car and she must have said something that acted as a trigger for an unhealed wound, or perhaps it was just another of her unthinking put-downs. As she was speaking, and as I was battening down my inner defences, we passed a neon advertisement for a brand of beer. It was flashing the word 'courage'. If there are such things as signs and portents, they probably appear in the most prosaic form. This one, a beer advert, acted as an injection of pure grace, the grace that validated what I was feeling in that instant, in that present moment, and in all the experiences from which it had sprung. It served as a kind of advocacy over and against the damage that was still being done by a narcissistic parent. It was an injection of pure energy, a graced 'touch', the breath I needed to take in order to carry on remembering clearly and truthfully.

When running a race, or embarking on what seems like an impossible task, you take a breath first. As with a race, or any action involving reserves of energy, will, and courage, you might take half a step back in order to be propelled forward by the added spring or energy that the backward step, or deeper breath has given you. You take a step back into those memories. I think we are doing this most of the time as we look back over our lives and try to make sense of them, trying to see what the connections were and if they meant anything, trying to put our shattered selves back together again, to make a composite picture using the missing pieces, or the gaps they create, to give a shape to the whole.

To remember aright is an impossible task, or so it seems to begin with. It is a race you are running against your own life. You must speak the story and have it heard as truth. That is the race. Sometimes you don't see a connection, or understand its meaning, until years after the moment has passed. Sometimes you wish you had understood it better in the moment of its happening. It could have changed the way you saw another person. It could have changed your life, perhaps.

So I do not think we can make sense of our lives by returning to the beginning and attempting to either recall, or put together, the missing pieces in their correct sequence. The missing pieces are probably hidden in the middle somewhere, and the middle is where we are living right now. Right now is the sum total of all our missing memories, a rich reserve from which to create not only life for ourselves but for others. Our trauma is always connected to someone else's. While a person who has experienced abuse will not necessarily become an abuser, if they are vulnerable for any reason, abuse or violence may have been the only way they have been able to survive in a family or group context. The victims of trauma and abuse are victims by virtue of their being in the category marked 'OK to abuse'. They will be black, or women, or children, or a person with learning disabilities, or anyone who is denied a voice, or reckoned to be invisible by those who abuse them, whether the abuse is physical or emotional, deliberate or barely conscious.

The missing memories may also be part of someone else's trauma which in turn is connected to the greater whole of history, and of our own history, if we get to know the persons concerned. I think this is particularly relevant in regard to historic trauma. We are all part of a bigger picture. I remember, as I write this, my visit to Rafi's parents who lived in East Jerusalem at the time, while it was still Palestinian. They had a woman to help around the house. She had lost an eye in the massacre that took place at Der Yassin in 1948. She and Rafi's parents were the bearers of collective trauma. They were witnesses. To witness to something is to consciously abide in it, so that others might not forget what has happened to a community or nation in the context of war.[12] Rafi's parents, who had lost their house and their land,

---

[12] The meaning and purpose of witness in relation to trauma is a complex subject but well worth pursuing further. For an account of

were witnessing to the collective trauma being experienced by Palestinians as they lived with their own personal trauma of the loss of their home and lands. Visiting them, and getting to know them, brought their suffering into the present moment, not because they talked about it, but because of a graced endurance which did not compromise their understanding of the injustice they had experienced or of who and what they were as Palestinians. The present moment, the one I was in as I met and got to know them, was graced by their graced endurance of their own suffering. That grace enabled love to be established between us, rather than distrust. Anyone visiting them would have also been made acutely conscious of the line that separates the trauma of a moment from the suffering that will endure from that moment into a person or a community's life. Theirs was also a repetition of trauma.

Repetition of trauma is the stuff of history. Trauma has to be witnessed to, survived and, where possible, transfigured across multiple generations. Second generation holocaust survivors will have to constantly balance what Eva Hoffman

---

cross-generational witness in the context of the *Shoa* see, for example, Eva Hauffman's *After Such Knowledge: A Meditation on the Aftermath of the Holocaust* (London: Random House, 2004) For a theological breakdown of the significance of witness, understood as a form of bearing the pain of past events, both personal and collective, see Shelly Rambo *Spirit and Trauma: A Theology of Remaining*, (Louisville: John Knox Press, 2010)

calls 'the twinned imperatives of loyalty and hate'.[13] Palestinians will mirror this obligation, almost as if their people's experience of genocide and displacement was meant to re-tell, or re-figure, the trauma story of those for whom the State of Israel was created. They are being forced to carry on bearing that particular history-searing event in their own history, so that their own history becomes a kind of holocaust in its own right, a sacrificial burnt offering through which some kind of atonement is being worked. So much of the trauma that is experienced, whether by nations or individuals, has something of payback to it. It follows that in every present moment of trauma there is a future trauma, with its consequent suffering, waiting to happen somewhere, whether it be in the context of nations or of families.

So there is a sense in which the present, which is eternal, insofar as it pertains to this section of time and eternity that we happen to be experiencing right now, is also 'mid-time'. It is somewhere in the middle of the story, our own or that of a nation or group, and it is where we are positioned right now. The moment that is right now contains the beginning and creates space for the end. By space I mean the kind of experience that leaves something of itself behind, not just as a memory, but as the means for giving shape to the whole. We

---

[13] *After Such Knowledge* p.14

will only see this shape clearly when we get to the end of the story of our lives, although we may get glimpses of it before then. So we try to make this mid-time as rich as possible, making the best of life as we know it today while also remembering the past. We try to live at our best in whatever we are experiencing today, in this present moment, which is the sum total of all our other moments and experiences.

On looking back at my own life, I see how these moments are connected and ultimately beginning to be shaped into a life which defies what I had been led to expect, growing up between a narcissistic mother, an abusive stepfather and an absentee father. There has been a connecting thread which has sustained me in life and ultimately given that life a shape and a meaning. The thread has been oxygen. Oxygen, like water, fills whatever space is available to it, so I have found that the more I can create space for this oxygen of life to fill, the more fruitful my own life has become. Creating space has been about owning the truthfulness of the past and now finding that I have, in a sense, been given permission to write about it.[14]

---

[14] I am personally indebted to Susan Brison for the confidence that enables me to write in the first person and which I believe is essential if trauma stories are not to be reduced to mere theories at the service of theology or of any other academic discipline.

I could pick up on any moment of my life as I have told it thus far and trace the 'touch', the connecting, the encounter that shaped the rest of it. I do not have to continue in a forward movement or keep looking backwards. The moment is here and the connection is now. I could light on other moments that have occurred randomly over the years when I realise there have been unexpected, unrecognised encounters with something, or someone, who set me on a new course. I cannot say exactly when these might have occurred. They belong with the half-remembered events, good and bad, that make up a life. Perhaps the kind of encounter they embody was already happening in those half-remembered moments of unmerited pain.

The kind of encounter I'm describing can remain buried beneath the surface of our consciousness, as an unspoken memory that may be resurrected in one of those *déjà vu* moments, through the subconscious associations we experience in a piece of music or a particular smell, or the snatch of a conversation. These are moments when something is suddenly known, when the pieces are put together, when we remember what the association is.

The things that trigger the associations often turn out to be quite inconsequential. At other times it is the act of trying to remember, of trying to get at the truth, that resonates with a deeper need for something or someone greater than we are who knows us profoundly and loves us. This greater person holds the truth of who we are, what happened to us, what might have happened to us, and is present to us in all the different ways we think of ourselves. The most difficult thing for a trauma survivor to accept is the fact that we are known in this way, that all the possibilities are known and that we are loved, that we are even loveable. We are completely loveable in being who we are with all that we may have experienced and what those experiences have done to us. For those who have endured abuse, both emotional and sexual, it is the hardest thing to accept because it runs counter to what the abuse has conditioned them to believe about themselves.

As the daughter of a narcissistic mother I know that I was in a sense complicit with her behaviour. I played along with it by laughing with her at the person she wanted me to be, and by being that person. It was safer in the long run to remain in that place because it required nothing of me. There were no expectations from either of my parents that I would be anything other than what they assumed, and possibly wanted, me to be. This is all part of the trauma that many people, especially women, learn to absorb and adapt to in later life.

Most of us never wake up to what it has deprived us of until much later. We give up on our responsibility to ourselves.

We give up on our giftedness and on any hopes we might have of making something of them. We are, after all, not worth it. We are not loveable even though we may long to feel that we are. Perhaps we felt this need to know ourselves as loveable in the earliest instances of life itself, in the first cry we uttered as we emerged from our mother's body, from darkness into light; too much light, perhaps, light against which the fragile nascent self has no defences.

The urge to sleep, at day's end, or when we are tired or stressed, is, I believe, an urge to return to this original dark safe place, away from too much light. Little research has been done about how safe this place really feels for the foetus, the extent to which she or he experiences fear, or peace, or even love, but it is a place of returning, a place where the good darkness takes into itself the dark times that were not so good.

Here, I recall two moments of returning to that dark place; a moment of discovering myself to be alone in my uncle's house in Paris, and of returning to my safe inner space; another of being lost while riding in the Spanish countryside. I had been lent a horse so that I could explore the estate we were visiting. I think it is only in the company of a creature that one really meets a landscape, in the way you meet a person when your hand touches theirs and there is an eye-to-eye engagement. The land had a visceral quality to it, an inner power which felt alien and somehow frightening. There was a physical connection between the ground and the unshod horse which I could feel through the reins, as if it was I who was picking my way through the stones and the red earth. The heat was physical too, as were the flies as the day drew to a close. There came a point when it felt right to head back to the house but I had no idea where I was. I did not know the terrain or the geography, but the horse was intelligent and kind and got us both home before it was completely dark.

The encroaching darkness, and being completely lost, touched on a different kind of darkness that we experience when we lose touch with the possibility that we matter or even exist. The darkness was, in a sense, the only reality. It was almost as if I did not exist at all. It evoked a reality that all abuse victims must engage with and find a way through, a way of trusting that we will come through our own personal darkness if we are willing to trust the Other who we call God, to surrender control. Being lost in the encroaching darkness in a terrain that was completely unknown to me meant that I had to trust the horse. He was all I had. So it was a case of simply letting go of the reins and giving the horse his head, of allowing him to turn away from the sun, away from the light, trusting that he knew his way home. He did. It was a profound connection involving physical contact. It involved touch. The connection was made from my body to his and through having to surrender everything to the instinct of that horse. Those who have experienced trauma or abuse need to be prepared to do this surrendering, to surrender to a loving God, especially in the dark times.

In the few hours intervening between Christ's appearance before the High Priest and his trial before Pontius Pilate, he was lowered into a holding cell. The cell would have been a dark pit into which the prisoner was lowered with ropes. Jesus would have been able to see the stars and then the gradually awakening day through the hole above his head as he waited to be taken to Pilate. He would have been watching for the light which, though lightening the darkness of his cell would also signal his impending death. It reminds me of the words of the psalm which I often reach for in dark times 'The darkness is not dark to you. The night is as bright as the day.' (Ps. 139:12) I wonder if Jesus prayed that psalm during the hours he spent in that cell. Had he reached a point beyond trust? Is it possible in such a situation to surrender to what is happening to you and to trust? Was he meeting the abuse victim in situations where they have no choice but to surrender? Was he in solidarity with them in a lifetime of depression that would follow, in which they would have to allow themselves to be touched by him and so re-learn trust?

The story of Christ being lowered into a pit, and the hours he might have spent there, resonates with depression. It also serves as a description of Christ's descent into Hell, which we affirm in the Creed, that middle-time period between his death and rising again. Artists through the ages have depicted Hell in all its horrors in a number of ways, often as a moral abyss, or, like Hieronymus Bosch, as the kind of place Christ might have visited in order to redeem lost souls from the clutches of Satan. Others have painted it in less graphic terms. Some artists may have been experiencing a private hell in themselves and sought to echo or resolve it through their paintings. I think of Edvard Munch's 'The Scream' and much of Francis Bacon's work which repeatedly visits the hellish worlds of inner fragmentation and loss of self. Other artists, like Samuel Palmer, Paul Gauguin and Mark Rothko, who were also going through hell, resist it in their work, dwelling on the light in delicate depictions of truth, through landscape or solid walls of colour. I think that all these artists are, in some measure, present to the Christ who is in Hell, who enters into the private claustrophobia of depression that many of us endure as a result of trauma or abuse. Where Christ is present, depression is no longer a private hell, even if it ultimately seems to defeat us, as it sometimes does. Rothko was an artist of deep faith who committed suicide. There is no conditional dividing line between depression and mental stability, or between depression and faith itself. The edges can blur very easily.

The worst thing about depression is that it seems to pertain exclusively to the person who is experiencing it. Each person experiences depression in a unique way. Each of us is in our own holding cell, looking up at the dark sky, waiting for the light to appear. Depression is not just a medical condition which has various names, depending on its severity. Whatever its name, depression shapes itself to the person and to where they are, to what they may or may not be doing in the present moment. It shapes itself to us in a suffocating way. Some people literally cannot breathe when they are experiencing severe depression. But even if depression allows us to breathe physically, it invariably stifles any other kind of breathing, making it impossible to function creatively, to love, to have anything left of our private selves to give to others. Depression reduces the self almost to non-existence. This I think is the hell that Christ visited at various points in his life and, according to the Creeds, on Holy Saturday, the intervening time between his death and rising again.

But what is the purpose of Christ's descent into Hell? What part does it play in the redemptive process, especially for those who have experienced abuse? Before we can even begin to answer this question, I think that Christ's experience of the total abandonment of being completely dead and in Hell gives us permission to allow for the fact that a hell exists. I use the word exist reservedly since I do not see hell itself as limited to a physical place in which things exist. Human beings are quite capable of turning physical space into a hell, for themselves or, as we are seeing through the effects of what we have done to the planet, for other human beings and for other species. Hell is a dimension, one that we have all experienced to a greater or lesser degree. Hell shapes itself around us according to context and circumstance. For this reason, it is impossible to compare one person's hell with another's. The horrors of Verdun or Auschwitz bear no relation to our depression, or even to being the victim of violent sexual abuse, but depression puts us in that spiritual dimension.

Depression can also be generated by other hells a person may have endured, especially those involving violence. However we choose to think of Hell, Christ's descent there was, I believe, real. The spirit of the dead man Jesus went somewhere on Holy Saturday. For those of us who suffer from depression I think we can safely bet that his spirit went to meet ours in these times of darkness. He embraced the sense of dislocation and severance from reality that we can feel in times of depression. From what I have learned and read about extreme forms of depression, it seems that in such

185

times you become 'severed' from your body, quite separate from it, without any sense of obligation to it. At times, it seems that you could leave it or return to it at will, as I thought I could do when I took the paracetamol. The body of the suicidal man or woman is lying there alongside the entombed Christ readying itself for its descent into Hell where Christ goes on ahead to meet the suicide victim. Here, I do not imply that a person who commits suicide is condemned to Hell.

The theologians Hans Urs Von Balthasar and Adrienne von Speyer describe Christ's descent into Hell as a bridge-building exercise.[15] The bridge compares with the kind of rope bridge deployed in military campaigns in impenetrable tropical forests. There is a deep ravine into which Christ descends, but a rope is thrown across the ravine for us to walk across. Who throws the rope? Not the disappeared Christ, but his 'abiding' spirit, his 'witnessing' spirit. To witness to something is to remain in it, rather than to merely speak of it. Real empathy with another person involves remaining with them in whatever they are enduring. It involves embracing the reality they are having to embrace and their helplessness in it. Christ is really dead. He is not in a position to throw ropes or to be of any help to anyone, least of all to himself,

---

[15] Hans Urs von Balthaser, *Heart of the World* in *Aftermath* in Shelly Rambo, *Spirit and Trauma*, ch. 2

but he encounters us in our helplessness, in that strange power that we call his Spirit. We are not alone in our hells.

These stories and interpretations of Christ's encounter with the deepest kind of depressive darkness help me to make sense of depression and of the trigger memories that relate to abuse. They do not invite 'belief' in the way that word is often thought to mean, but act as 'guides' and supports in times of inner disintegration, darkness and confusion. Christ's descent into Hell becomes our descent into Hell, so we are not alone in it. In other words, we do not become our depression. Depression is not who we are. So there is a transition to be effected which is often quite difficult. It involves being in a conceptual space, an inner place, in which we encounter Christ and allow him to embody us, especially when we are at our weakest. I have found my own darkest moments to have been times of Christ embodiment, although I only realised them as such much later in life. In these darkest of times I was returned to the choice I faced at the point in my childhood when it was as if I was being asked whether I wanted my life to turn out like my mother's, whether I wanted to live as she did or become the kind of person she was.

I am very like my mother, so it was a difficult question to have to face. Ultimately, it amounted to a matter of wanting or not wanting to live at all. In the realisation that I did want to live and not destroy myself, or the lives of others who might depend on me in the future, I had to think myself into a place where it was conceivable that some greater Other was able to re-frame me, and my life, according to quite different precepts, One I could inhabit and who could inhabit me, so becoming the bridge over the abyss of depression.

We have Christ and we have the bridge of his Spirit to walk on so that we can cross the abyss. The darkness of the abyss itself, for us, consists only in refusing the offer of the bridge, in refusing God's love, because our depression and our experience of abuse tells us that we are not worthy of it, or that it simply does not exist.

I was in this place as I broke away from Rafi. I walked the New York streets in the sweltering summer heat of 1973 in the way I had walked the streets of Paris, trying to make sense of my life and in search of something or someone who would not think me a total failure. Failure had taken on a whole new meaning. A failed marriage, even if it should not have taken place at all, leaves you with a failed life. It is not just a matter of the past. The future seems failed before it has even happened. I did not have the emotional strength to deal with this realisation, so it was a question of fight or flight. Either I would fight it with drugs or I would run from it. So I ran. I returned to Ibiza, to sun-baked beaches, to the parties, to the all-pervading presence of Spain's lingering fascism, glimpsed in officialdom, overheard in chance remarks, felt at my mother's dinner parties in the stunned silence that accompanied her suggestion that we raise our glasses to Franco.

Life is textured and variegated. In the midst of darkness there is light. It is also when darkness calls itself light that we witness, or are made party to, the greatest evil. We live with spiritual conflict, most of the time completely unaware of it. We live in dark places where the light insists on entering and overcoming the darkness, through events that some would call coincidences, but which are better thought of as having to do with the graced purposes of a loving God.

Through my own tears I glimpsed a memory of two brothers back in the UK. The elder one had enormous charm and an Aston Martin DB5. The three of us had had fun. My mother had, through coincidence or through graced purpose, rescued the younger one from a beach in Ibiza where he and a friend were living on hard boiled eggs and tomatoes. He was talented, funny, unpredictable, and solid as a rock. I was ready to move forward, to commit. I wanted his children. I married him.

Appendix

For further reflection

Chapter 1

To understand is to forgive. Do you agree? Should Christians always forgive? Why?

What is your earliest memory of separation? Were you comforted or supported in it?

How did you feel about yourself at the time? Did you feel worthless? Did you feel betrayed?

Did you have a religious upbringing? Who shaped your earliest ideas about God?

Did you feel that you deserved God's love? Did you feel you deserved your parents' love?

As a result of reading this chapter, what does 'remembering aright' mean for you now?

Chapter 2

Was there a Christ figure in your life? Did they try to protect you? How do you feel about them now?

What was your social/cultural context? Upper, lower, middle class, BAME? How did your class context affect the way you were treated and how you felt about others?

As a child, what was your experience of adult anger (if any)?

Did you experience not belonging? How did (or does) that affect the way you relate to others, especially in a group or family context?

Are children innocent?

If you experienced any form of abuse (sexual, physical, emotional or spiritual), is your abuser still alive? What would you like to say to them now?

Are you drawn to powerful people? Why? (question applies to both a 'yes' or a 'no' answer)

Are you drawn to controlling people?

When did you first experience shame? Were you obliged to say nothing? Was the truth of what caused you to feel ashamed denied you (i.e. 'gaslighting')?

Chapter 3

Were either of your parents alcoholics or addicted? How did that affect your relationship with them?

What did you most need from your parents – and failed to receive?

What is your experience of narcissistic parenting?

Failing your children is the ultimate failure. Do you agree?

Looking back at your darkest times, can you discern a Christ presence 'roading' with you?

Have you ever felt honoured?

Chapter 4

Have you ever felt completely alone, as opposed to lonely?

If you have children, has your own experience of trauma affected how you relate to them?

Have you ever felt the need for 'payback'?

Has your experience of trauma informed the way you think about God?

Do you believe in your own goodness?

Do you have a focal point for prayer, e.g. an icon or picture?

Could you allow God to contemplate you?

Chapter 5

Do you know what it feels like not to be believed? If so, how does the experience of not being believed inform your sense of self? Do you believe in yourself and in the truth of your experience? If you have ceased to believe in your own truth, how do you think that has happened?

Do you have a need for reassurance and affirmation? To what extent does that affect the work you do and your relationships?

Did you experience rejection as a child? How do you deal with rejection now?

Do you deny your own giftedness?

Do you ever experience the 'pull of God'?

Chapter 6

Have you had your own intelligence denied to you? Do you deny it to yourself?

Have you ever felt loved, or been told you are good, clever or beautiful by someone who loves you? Can you imagine God feeling this way about you?

Have you ever experienced what it feels like not to be taken seriously?

Can you remember the exact moment when trust was broken in regard to your relationship with your abuser?

Has this book helped you to allow 'touch points' to surface, so that grace can be worked into them?

Printed in Great Britain
by Amazon

86752951R00112